101 CHILIES
TO TRY BEFORE YOU DIE

101 CHILIES
TO TRY BEFORE YOU DIE

DAVID FLOYD

FIREFLY BOOKS

Chili heat levels

There are no official classifications for the heat levels in chili peppers, which are usually measured by Scoville heat units (SHU), but these are the categories I use and the way that this book has been organized.

0 SHU Sweet
0–2,500 SHU Mild
2,500–100,000 SHU Warm
100,000–500,000 SHU Hot
500,000–1,000,000 SHU Very Hot
1,000,000+ SHU Superhot

A FIREFLY BOOK

Published by Firefly Books Ltd. 2016

Text copyright © 2016 David Floyd
Design and layout copyright © 2016 Octopus Publishing Group

First printing

Publisher Cataloging-in-Publication Data (U.S.)

Names: Floyd, David, 1961-. author.
Title: 101 chilies to try before you die / David Floyd.
Description: Richmond Hill, Ontario, Canada : Firefly Books, 2016. | Summary: "101 Chilies to Try Before You Die has an intuitive list of exactly 101 chilies that range from sweet and mild to superhot, allowing the reader to work their way up to trying the hottest chilies known to man. Each chili is accompanied with a list of seed suppliers, ideal growing conditions, and a brief history of the chili itself" — Provided by publisher.
Identifiers: ISBN 978-1-77085-743-8 (hardcover)
Subjects: LCSH: Hot peppers. | Peppers. | Cooking (Peppers).
Classification: LCC SB351.P4F569 |DDC 633.84 – dc23

Library and Archives Canada Cataloguing in Publication

A CIP record for this title is available from Library and Archives Canada

Published in the United States by
Firefly Books (U.S.) Inc.
P.O. Box 1338, Ellicott Station
Buffalo, New York 14205

Published in Canada by
Firefly Books Ltd.
50 Staples Avenue, Unit 1
Richmond Hill, Ontario L4B 0A7

Printed and bound in China

Conceived, designed, and produced by
by Cassell Illustrated, a division of
Octopus Publishing Group Ltd
Carmelite House
50 Victoria Embankment
London EC4Y 0DZ
David Floyd asserts the moral right to be identified as the author of this work.

Senior Commissioning Editor: Eleanor Maxfield
Editor Pauline Bache
Copyeditor Jane Birch
Designers Jeremy Tilston and Jaz Bahra
Picture Research Manager
Giulia Hetherington
Picture Library Manager Jen Veall
Assistant Production Manager: Caroline Alberti

Contents

Introduction

Welcome to the world of fire and spice. Chilies and peppers are one of the fastest-growing areas in food with new brands and products launched all the time. Luckily, we can almost all grow chilies at home, even if we have only a windowsill and a few small flowerpots.

Because this book tries to cover as wide a range of chilies as possible, I have not just selected the hottest 101 chilies I could find—while being macho they would also be boring. So we start with some mild peppers and work our way up via interesting variations to the latest superhot chilies.

I hope along the way to show you to some new tastes and chili styles that impressed me over the last 20 years working with chilies. I was first introduced to chilies in a big way when my career took me on frequent trips to California, where it was deemed fun to try to kill the Brit with the hottest Thai and Mexican food that they could find. Each time I returned home I would bring new sauces, dried chilies, and recipes back to try on my friends.

During the years, I have manufactured barbeque rubs, had my own brand of chili-flavored potato chips and chili flavorings, sold chili ice cream, written books and articles, and run a successful online chili store and probably the world's largest chili blog (www.chilefoundry.co.uk).

I hope you enjoy this book as much as I did researching it over the past 20-plus years.

The common chili species

There are currently only five commonly grown chili species that we describe as cultivated, but there are many more wild species and maybe a few yet to be discovered. The common species are:

Capsicum annuum This is the most popular of the cultivated species; the name comes from the mistaken idea that these are annuals and have to be grown each year. Examples include: Aleppo Pepper (see page 84), NuMex Heritage Big Jim (see page 86), Pepperdew™ Piquanté Pepper (see page 38), Jalapeño (see page 60), and Poblano (Ancho) and Mulato (see page 34).

Capsicum chinense Named by Dutch botanist Nikolaus Joseph von Jacquin in 1776, who believed they originated from China. Examples include: Carolina Reaper (see page 220), Orange Habanero (see page 178),

Scotch Bonnet (see page 180), and Bhut Jolokia (see page 200).

Capsicum baccatum The name "baccatum" comes from the word *baccate*, which means berrylike; it is probably one of the first domesticated species of chilies, with evidence dating it back to the Incas. Examples include: Ají Amarillo (see page 116) and Criolla Sella (see page 98).

Capsicum frutescens Often combined with *C. annuum*, but research by Paul G. Smith and Charles B. Heiser Jr. in 1957 identified this as a separate species, although it can take an expert to tell them apart. Examples include: Prik Kee Nu (see page 168), Tabasco (see page 126), and Siling Labuyo (see page 158).

Capsicum pubescens The name "pubescens" refers to the small hairs found on the underside of the leaves and stems, so pubescens means "hairy." Uniquely, if you cut a pod open, you will find the seeds of this species are black or dark brown. They will also not crossbreed with the other cultivated species. The flowers are a blue/violet color. Examples include: Rocoto (see page 94).

Wild chilies

There are currently 26 species that are described as wild chilies. There is little published research on these and I am sure there will be some duplication as well as some new ones to be found.

Known wild chili species include: *Capsicum buforum, C. cattingae, C. campylopodium, C. cardenasii/ulupica, C. chacoense, C. cornutum, C. dimorphum, C. dusenii, C. exile, C. eximium, C. galapaqoense, C. geninifolium, C. hookerianum, C. lanceolatum, C. leptopdum, C. longidentatum, C. minutiflorum, C. mirabile, C. parvifolium, C. praetermissum, C. rhomboideum, C. scottianum, C. scolnikianum, C. tovarii,* and *C. villosum.*

Each of these species comes from different regions of South America, with the exception of the *C. galapaqoense,* which comes from the Galapagos Islands. There is a growing interest in wild chilies and you can often find seeds on specialty websites, including www.fataliiseeds.net and www.tradewindsfruit.com

Some key terms

Open-pollination is the natural process by which insects, etc. pollinate the plants. If you are growing a single variety without other varieties nearby, you will probably get seeds that are descended from parents of the same strain of the species, but it is not guaranteed.

Closed/controlled pollination is what commercial seed producers do to make sure the seeds they produce stay true to the breed. To make sure there is no cross-pollination, they keep the plants isolated while the flowers form. Once the flowers drop and the pods start to grow, the seeds should be safely uncrossed. This does mean that the producers may have to pollinate the plants manually using a soft brush or cotton swab to move the pollen from the male to female parts of the flowers. Cross-pollination will have no effect on the pods you produce from a plant; it will affect only the seeds and therefore subsequent generations.

Dehybridization If you want to create your own open-pollinated variety or cultivar (short for cultivated variety) from an F1 hybrid (see opposite) it is possible, but the process can be time-consuming and good results are not guaranteed. To dehybridize a plant, you will need to collect seeds from many generations, each time carefully selecting only the plants with the characteristics you desire.

Some commercial crops are developed to have characteristics that are desirable to commercial growers, such as having all the pods ripen at a similar time to help with harvesting. However, the domestic grower may prefer to have a long sustained harvest so they can use the chilies over the season as they ripen.

The Super Chili is an F1 hybrid that has been successful with the domestic grower, but over the last few years an open-pollinated variety called Super Tramp has been developed (see page 134). It shares many of the good characteristics of the Super Chili, such as its tolerance to shade, quick maturity, and high productivity, making it ideal for the home grower.

Heirloom and heritage varieties You will see some chilies described as heirloom and heritage varieties. There is not a strict definition of what makes a plant an heirloom or heritage variety, but it does indicate that the plant is an open-pollinated variety that has been maintained over time by growers who appreciate its unique properties. Seeds of heirloom and heritage chilies have been carefully passed down through generations of growers. The history of these varieties is hard to trace to a single point, but they mostly come from ethnic groups or communities. Heirloom plants generally survive because they have become well-suited to the conditions in a region or they show a particular variation that is valued by the grower. Now these varieties are being sought after, because most lack the uniformity and blandness that modern crossbreeding has created.

Hangjiao Translating to "space pepper," these are seeds associated with the Chinese space rocket Shijian-8, launched in 2006 with around 2,000 seeds, including peppers and chilies, some of which showed improvements in size, taste, or nutritional value on their return. There seems to be no definitive explanation why a short trip to space alters these seeds, but they were exposed to cosmic radiation, zero gravity, and changing magnetic fields.

F1 hybrid An F1 hybrid is created whenever you cross any two stable chili varieties, the resulting plant being called an F1. Seeds from this plant would create an F2 hybrid. F2 hybrids are more unstable and this is why most of the time saving seeds from an F1 hybrid is not recommended.

The Slow Food Foundation Ark of Taste This is a database of small-scale produce, including chilies and peppers, that are under threat of being lost in an increasingly homogenized world. You can search the Ark of Taste at www.fondazioneslowfood.com/en/ark-of-taste-slow-food/ and have a look at what needs saving near you.

Seed saver groups There are a number of groups opening up in forums and on social media. On a more professional level, there is also the Seed Savers Exchange (www.seedsavers.org), a nonprofit organization that shares seeds from a huge range of plants, including chilies. Note that, when using their website, you need to look under "peppers," as sweet peppers and chilies are classified together. There is a minimum order for free shipping, but you can group together with other chilie fans if you have a small order. The selection of seeds is amazing and it is one of the few places where you can get the Hussli Tomato Pepper (see page 30) as well as many other rare species.

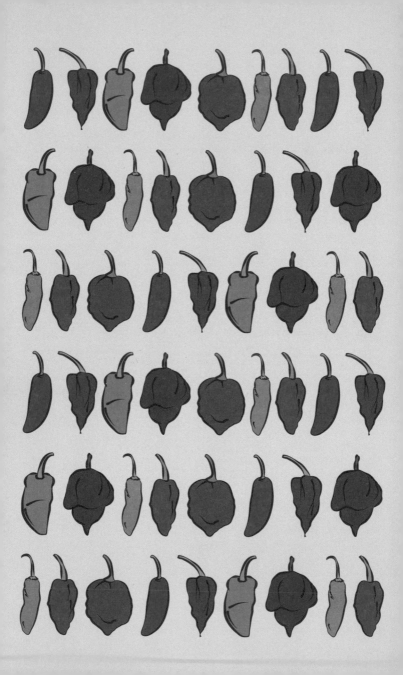

Sweet & Mild

Jimmy Nardello

Tomato Pepper

Spike & Joker

Zavory Pepper

Cubanelle

Chilhuacle Negro

Apricot Habanero

Beaver Dam Pepper

Biquinho

Hussli Tomato Pepper

Anaheim

Poblano (Ancho) & Mulato

Paprika

Peppadew™ Piquanté Pepper

Pimientos de Padrón

Cascabel

Kashmiri Mirch

Cherry Bomb

Guajillo

Purple Tiger

Bulgarian Carrot

Hungarian Hot Wax

Bishop's Hat

1

Jimmy Nardello

SPECIES

C. annuum

POD DESCRIPTION

Pods are 6–8 inches long
and ¾–1½ inches wide,
turning from green to
a bright, shiny red.

GROWING INFO

Very productive, well
worth growing but
will need a greenhouse
or hoop house in cool
climates.

SEED SUPPLIERS

BCS, MWCH, PSEU,
PZW, SLP, TWF

How wonderful would it be to have a pepper
cultivar named after you and saved for future
generations. That is what has happened to Jimmy
Nardello, whose pepper seeds are being kept in
climate-controlled conditions by the Seed Savers
Exchange in Decorah, Iowa (see page 9).

Originally from the Basilicata region of
Italy, these peppers were the favorites of
Angela Nardello who, with her husband
Giuseppe and young daughter Anna, set sail
for the United States in 1887 from Naples. They
eventually settled in Naugatuck, a small town
in Connecticut.

Jimmy was the family's fourth child of 11 and
shared Angela's love of gardening. He passed
away in 1983, but not before donating some of his
pepper seeds to the Seed Savers Exchange.

For such a short plant, at only 1 foot 8 inches—
2 feet high, they produce a good crop of long,
thin-skinned pods.

SCOVILLE
RATING

0
SHU

2   Tomato Pepper

SPECIES
....
C. annuum

SCOVILLE
RATING

**0–50,000
SHU**

Surprisingly, there are a number of Tomato Pepper varieties. Their claim to fame is that they have more than a passing resemblance to a tomato. As you can see from the picture, they more than just resemble tomatoes—the quick way to tell the difference between the two is to look at the calyx and stem. Once cut open, the Tomato Pepper is much like any other chili variety.

Records of this style of chili date back to 1613, when respected apothecary and botanist Basilius Besler illustrated a cherry pepper that looked especially like a tomato in shape.

Tomato Peppers split into two main shapes: there are small, round, tomato-shaped pods, such as the Weaver's Mennonite, Bombita F1, and the Ciliegia Piccante (aka Baccio de Satana or Satan's Kiss), and the larger Red Ruffled Pimiento and the Italian Topepo Rosso, both of which are sweet peppers that look more like beefsteak tomatoes.

The Red Ruffled Pimiento produces beautiful 2½–4-inch-wide pods with thick flesh that ripens to a deep scarlet color, whereas the Topepo Rosso is one of the best-flavored sweet peppers.

The oddly named Sheepnose Pimento has the look of an overstuffed tomato but has also been described as having an apple shape. Although strictly a sweet pepper, it has been included in the Slow Food Foundation Ark of Taste (see page 9).

POD DESCRIPTION

There are two main shapes: small, round, tomato-shaped pods and those that look more like beefsteak tomatoes. Both styles will ripen to a red color to help with the tomato illusion.

GROWING INFO

Tomato peppers are easy to grow, but check the description on the seed supplier site, because some are more hardy than others.

SEED SUPPLIERS

HS, LS, NN

3

Spike & Joker

SPECIES

C. annuum

POD DESCRIPTION

The upright, thin, spiky pods ripen from green to red, growing to ¾–1½ inches long and just fractions of an inch wide.

GROWING INFO

If you have one of these varieties, I think you must also grow the other. If you keep them in a small flowerpot, you will keep the plant small and manageable, but it can take a while for the plant to mature and start producing.

SEED SUPPLIER

SSS

SCOVILLE
HEAT UNITS

0–100,000
SHU

Spike and Joker are two separate varieties that have been developed from the same cross.

Spike is a low, bushy variety that produces thousands of thin, elongated, pointed miniature pods that stick upward from the plant, hence the name. Spike is best described as a vigorous grower and it will grow to fill any space you give it. A larger flowerpot means a larger plant. The chili pods are very hot, measuring up to 100,000 SHU. Thus, this variety is ideal for the home gardener/cook and it is superb as a house plant in a small flowerpot and impressive in a larger space in a greenhouse.

Joker is identical in appearance to Spike in every way—grown side by side, it is impossible to tell them apart. However, Joker has NO heat whatsoever; although it looks like a chili, it is heatless. This means that Joker is NOT a chili at all and, although it is tempting to call it a very mild chili, it is technically a sweet pepper.

As I understand it, Joker and Spike are genetically identical except for one gene, the gene that turns on the production of capsaicin. Joker, without the gene, is a sweet pepper, whereas Spike, with the gene, is a hot chili.

4

Zavory Pepper

SPECIES

C. chinense

POD DESCRIPTION

Bright red pods grow
a little larger than the
typical Habanero at
1¼–1½ inches wide and
2 inches long.

GROWING INFO

Like most Habaneros,
it can take a while to
germinate and needs a
long, warm summer to
ripen. It is slow to ripen,
and is best grown in a
greenhouse or under
a hoophouse in cool
climates.

SEED SUPPLIERS

BPC, CCN, SLP

SCOVILLE
RATING

10-100
SHU

Although a lot of time and effort have gone
into creating the superhot chilies, there are—
perhaps surprisingly and often overlooked in
our fascination with finding the hottest—other
growers who are expending the same time and
effort to make chilies milder, while trying to
retain the flavor of the hot variety. Zavory is one
such chili.

This mild, very much a Habanero-style chili
was developed by Dr. Paul Grun at Pennsylvania
State University.

The Zavory really does look like a fiery
Habanero, making it ideal for a few tricks to be
played on the unsuspecting. The plant grows to
2–2¼ feet high and can produce a good crop of
bright red pods.

There are other heatless Habanero-style
chilies and the Ají Dulce from Venezuela is
a popular variety, getting its name from the
Spanish for sweet, *dulce* (*ají* being "chili"). It is
grown commercially in Venezuela and is used in
the local version of the tamale called the hallaca.

You may think, why not just use a sweet bell
pepper? Why waste your time on these? These
chilies offer the flavors that make the Habanero
so popular and open a market for people who are
less tolerant of heat to enjoy them.

When I talk to even the most hardened
hotheads, they always mention the flavor that
the extreme chilies provide as being the reason
they eat them. Myself, as I get older, find the heat
kills the flavor more quickly.

5

Cubanelle

SPECIES

C. annuum

SCOVILLE
RATING

200–1,000
SHU

This chili is used in both Cuban and Puerto Rican cooking and in Italian cuisine. It is about as close as we get to a sweet bell pepper in this guide, but it is so much more.

The flavor is what you would hope of a good bell pepper, enhanced by the thinner flesh and mild heat. Cubanelles are truly excellent thinly sliced and added to a salad. The pods are mostly picked when still green, but they will get slightly hotter if left until they are completely mature and red.

The skin can be removed by roasting over an open flame and then carefully peeling with your fingers or the edge of a spoon. Do not wash the pods, because they will lose their smoky flavor. They can then be stored in olive oil. In Italy, they are known as the Frying Pepper and are simply split open, seeded, and lightly fried in olive oil.

This is one chili pepper that I would welcome to see replace the bell pepper on our supermarket shelves.

POD DESCRIPTION

The pods start green and mature through to red. They grow to 4 inches long and 1½ –2 inches wide, tapering to a blunt tip.

GROWING INFO

Don't grow bell peppers, grow this instead. Easy to grow, it is a low-maintenance plant that likes full sun.

SEED SUPPLIERS

LS, PJ, SLP

AKA

Ají Cubanela, Cubanella, Friarelli, Italian Frying Pepper, Pimiento de Cocinar.

USAGE

Slice and add to salads, or roast and store covered in olive oil.

6

Chilhuacle Negro

SPECIES

C. annuum

POD DESCRIPTION

The large pods start green and ripen to a dark brown—almost black. They are similar in shape to a bell pepper, if a little smaller at 2¾–4 inches long and 1¼–2 inches wide.

GROWING INFO

This is a large plant that will need some space. To completely ripen, it will need warm conditions, and in cold climates it will need to be in a hoop house to reach its full potential.

SEED SUPPLIERS

CCN, LS, NN, SLP

AKA

Chili Negro, Mexican Negro, Pasilla Bajio.

Like most big chilies, this is not going to set the world alight in heat, but the flavor carries more than just hints of warm chocolate with the sweet scent of a rich pipe tobacco and dark dried Christmas fruits.

Originally from the Mexican Oaxaca region, where it likes the warm and mild climate, Chiluacle Negro is used locally to make the Oaxaca version of the Mexican national dish, Mole Negro.

The Chilhuacle is listed in the Slow Food Foundation Ark of Taste (see page 9), because the high cost of growing it has meant a steady decline in its production. Seeds are available, although not common, but are well worth searching for.

Two other Chilhuacle chilies come from the same area of Mexico. The yellow variety is known as the Chilhuacle Amarillo and the Chilhuacle Rojo is red. Again, although not commonly available, these are well worth growing if you can, although they differ in flavor from the Negro.

SCOVILLE RATING

250–1,500
SHU

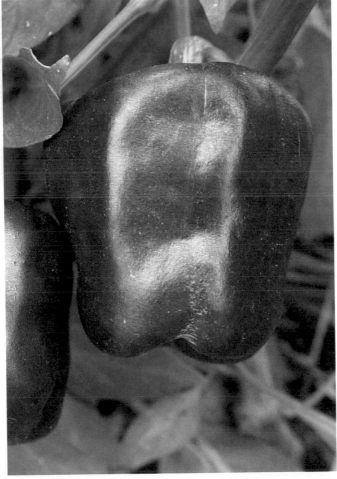

7

Apricot Habanero

Typically, the Habanero is something that the chili novice will avoid, since, although the flavor is great, the aftereffect of the heat takes some practice before it can be appreciated. There have been a number of mild or tamed chilies in the past, but often they lack more than just the heat—they seem to lack some of the flavors, too.

Fortunately, the Apricot Habanero has all the flavor and, especially, the aroma. In fact, it is a particularly fragrant variety—break open a single pod and everyone will know it. The heat level is extremely mild at only about 700 SHU; it is so mild that young children have eaten it without knowing it was a chili.

The plant is a prolific producer of beautifully even-shaped pods that ripen from lime green to a lovely salmon color. A great introduction to chilies, it can be grown in flowerpots or other containers or even directly in the ground.

Slice a few of these and add them to a strong cheddar cheese sandwich, or use them to make mild versions of any classic Mexican and Caribbean dishes.

SCOVILLE RATING

500–700 SHU

8

Beaver Dam Pepper

SPECIES

C. annuum

POD DESCRIPTION

The pods start lime green, maturing to red. They have a thick flesh and grow to about 8 inches long and 2½ inches wide, tapering to a point.

GROWING INFO

Should germinate well in a heated propagator. The plants can be grown in a large gardening grow bag filled with seeding and potting mix, but grow only one plant per bag , because they can grow large.

SEED SUPPLIERS

SLP, SS

USAGE

Ideal for use in fresh salsa; they are also big enough to stuff and, once completely ripe, can be dried and ground to make your own unique paprika. There is also a Beaver Dam Hot Sauce available.

Originally from Hungary and brought to the Beaver Dam, Wisconsin, area around 1912 by Joe Hussli, who was also responsible for the Hussli Tomato Pepper (see page 30) from the same area.

This pepper was almost lost until it was added to the Slow Food Foundation Ark of Taste list in 2007 (see page 9).

Since October 2014, there has been a Beaver Dam Pepper Festival to celebrate this pepper.

SCOVILLE RATING

500–1,000 SHU

9 Biquinho

SPECIES

C. chinense

SCOVILLE
RATING

500–1,000
SHU

From the Brazilian state of Minas Gerais comes Biquinho Pepper, which means "pepper beak" or "pepper pacifier," but it is also known as the Chupetinha or Pimenta Bico. The plant grows to about 1 foot 8 inches high and produces an abundance of small, red or yellow pods (dependent on the variety).

I have come across recipes for pickling these pods in vinegar and salt. Unexpectedly, the recipes blanched the pods in boiling water before rapidly cooling in iced water. This would have the effect of making the skin more porous and also of cleaning the pods, so it is less probable that they will spoil when pickled.

POD DESCRIPTION

Red or yellow pods that are ¾–1¼ inches in diameter. The pods are round with an elongated cone-shape beak or nipple on the base, making some of them almost a teardrop shape.

GROWING INFO

Compact plant with small pods, but likes warm conditions. Set your propagator to 72°F.

SEED SUPPLIERS

PBPC, SLP, SSS, TWF

AKA

Chupetinha, Pimenta Bico

10

Hussli Tomato Pepper

SPECIES

C. annuum

POD DESCRIPTION

The pepper grows to about 3¾ inches in diameter, features thick flesh, and ripens from green to orange and then to a deep red.

GROWING INFO

If you can find seeds, then grow them. If you like them, pass some on to your pals. Although these are open-pollinated (see page 8), the seeds don't always grow like their parents, because of cross-pollination with other nearby chilies. Seed producers work hard to keep plants from cross-pollinating.

SEED SUPPLIERS

None

This chili is a small, heavy pepper that gets its name from its visual resemblance to a traditional-style tomato.

It is believed to have been brought to the United States by Joe Hussli, who was also responsible for bringing the Beaver Dam Pepper (see page 26) to the same area around 1912.

Joe's family would sell this unique pepper only in its unripe green state so that the seeds would not be viable, thus making sure they had no competition. The latest grower in the family, Larry, has been growing them for more than 45 years, giving away most of what he grows. He has also shared the seeds with other interested growers, making sure this variety is not lost.

The Slow Food Foundation has selected this pepper for its Ark of Taste (see page 9), publicizing this pepper to a new group of people interested in food for the quality of the flavor, not just the ease of growth or the shelf life.

Hopefully, seeds for these will become available in seed catalogs and via online resellers, but at the moment you will have to search to find some and the best places would be the seed saver groups (see page 9).

SCOVILLE RATING

500–2,000 SHU

11 Anaheim

SPECIES

C. annuum

SCOVILLE
RATING

500–2,500 SHU

The Anaheim gets its name from the city of Anaheim, California, which today is probably better known for the number of theme parks than for the local agriculture. But in 1894, well before theme parks, Emilio C. Ortega introduced a chili to the area that grew so successfully that it became known as the Anaheim Pepper. Emilio preserved the peppers by fire-roasting them to remove the skins; they were then seeded and finally washed before canning. His business, Ortega, is still producing canned Anaheim chilies to this day, as well as many other products.

They mature from green to red but are most often used when still green. All the canned chilies produced by Ortega, including those sold in jars, are in the green stage of maturity.

The pods have a thick, waxy, waterproof skin that should be removed before use. Traditionally, the method is to roast them over an open fire (a barbeque grill is good for this) until the skins are burned and blistered, then seal them in a bag to let the heat continue to loosen the skin. When cooled, gently pull the burned skin away from the flesh. If you want to have a smoked flavor, do not wash off any remaining burned flecks of the skin. They are now ready to be used or preserved.

They are a great chili to stuff and can be used as an alternative to the Poblano chili (see page 34) to make the dish Chili Relleno (Spanish for "stuffed chili") in which the chili is stuffed with cheese and then coated in an egg batter and deep-fried.

POD DESCRIPTION

The Anaheim chili grows up to 10 inches long and 2 inches wide. It matures from green to red.

GROWING INFO

The plant can grow to almost 3 feet 3 inches high and is big and bushy. It needs to be kept moist if you want it to produce some nice big pods.

SEED SUPPLIERS

HS, LS, NN, PZW, SDCF, SLP, SS

AKA

California Chili, Magdalena, and, when completely matured and dried, Chili Seco del Norte.

USAGE

Excellent for stuffing.

12

Poblano (Ancho) & Mulato

SPECIES
....
C. annuum

SCOVILLE
RATING
....
500–3,000
SHU

The Poblano is a very mild chili from the Mexican state of Puebla, where *poblano* means "pepper from Puebla." The Poblano pods have a heart shape and can grow up to 3¼ by 6 inches; they have thick flesh and ripen from a dark green to a chocolate brown.

When dried, the Poblano changes its name to become the Ancho. It is available all year dried and can be found in most specialty retailers. I sometimes use it shredded up and then lightly dry-fried and added to my always-evolving chili con carne recipe.

Now comes the confusion. The Mulato and Poblano are basically the same; they are just different varieties of Poblano that produce darker or lighter pods. How they are categorized is decided when the pods are sorted. The dark brown, almost black, pods are graded as Mulato whereas, if they are dark brown with a hint of red, they are called Poblano/Ancho. The difference in pod color can depend on how long they are left to ripen.

Note: To add to the confusion, in some parts of southern California they call the Poblano a Pasilla, which elsewhere is a completely different variety.

POD DESCRIPTION

Mulato plants have dark brown pods whereas the Poblano/Ancho are lighter with a hint of red. They can grow to 2¾–6 inches long and 2–3 inches wide.

GROWING INFO

Best grown in the ground, these plants will need support, otherwise they will often break under the weight of the ripening pods. The plants grow tall, easily reaching 3 feet 3 inches high, and will need plenty of space.

SEED SUPPLIERS

BPC, BS, CB, CCN, CH, CSB, MWCH, NMSU, NN, PJ, PSEU, PZW, RMR, SDCF, SLP, SS, SSS, TCPC, TF, TWF, VNG

AKA

Pasilla (in southern California)

13 Paprika

SPECIES
....
C. annuum

SCOVILLE
RATING
....
500–10,000
SHU

Paprika is not a single chili pepper variety, but comes from a number of pepper varieties, all known for their strong red color.

When many people think of paprika, they think of Hungary, but Paprika is also grown in quantity in Spain, Serbia, and Holland (in large greenhouses), as well as in the United States. Although Hungary may be the home of paprika, Spain produces its own versions, in particular Pimentón de la Vera. This version has a smoky aroma, which comes from being dried and smoked using oak, with the whole process taking about 2 weeks.

Hungary takes paprika seriously. There is even a dedicated museum in the town of Szeged, which—with nearby Kalocsa—is the heart of Hungarian production. The industry became mechanized in 1859 when the Pálfy brothers from Szeged opened a Paprika mill that removed the seeds and membranes before grinding the pods.

In 1937, Hungarian scientist Dr. Szent-Györgyi was awarded the Nobel Prize for isolating vitamin C in Paprika. He also discovered that Paprika, and therefore chilies, contains more vitamin C than oranges.

Many varieties can be made into paprika, the common factor being the strength of the color. Look for known varieties, such as Leutschauer Paprika Pepper, Alma Paprika, and Dulce Rojo Paprika, which is a strong favorite, being mild and one of the easiest to grow.

POD DESCRIPTION

Each variety produces pods in different shapes, but all mature to the deep red needed for a classic paprika.

GROWING INFO

Loads of variation with the varieties, but they like a well-drained, fertile, and sunny position, and they are especially susceptible to frost.

SEED SUPPLIERS

BCS, CH, LS, PBPC, PJ, PSEU, PZW, RFC, SLP, SS, TCPC, TWF

AKA

Pimentón de la Vera

USAGE

Traditionally, the pods are air dried before grinding into powder.

14 Peppadew™ Piquanté Pepper

C. annuum

POD DESCRIPTION

The round pods grow to 1¼–1½ inches in diameter. They start green and mature via bright orange to red with a glossy skin and thick juicy flesh.

GROWING INFO

Successfully farmed on a huge scale in South Africa, so it should not be too hard to grow if you are able to find an official source of seeds.

SEED SUPPLIERS

HS (for Malawi Piquanté), RFC

USAGE

Pepperdew™ peppers available to buy have been processed and have the seeds removed before being preserved in a sweet solution.

SCOVILLE
RATING

900–1,100
SHU

The Pepperdew™ Piquanté Pepper is one of the few peppers for which you cannot officially buy seeds nor even grow your own plants. It was discovered growing in Port Elizabeth, South Africa, by farmer Johan Steenkamp in 1993. He cleverly recognized the potential of this pepper, collected the seeds, and developed his find into a stable chili that could be protected by PVP (Plant Variety Protection).

The PVP gives plant developers 25 years' protection. You cannot get it for any variety of chili; only new, distinct, uniform, and stable varieties (the Dorset Naga, see page 208, has also been through this rigorous process).

All the Pepperdew™ products are grown in the Limpopo and Mpumalanga provinces and the first products were introduced in 1996 in South Africa. Growing and processing are controlled by one company with strict growing contracts. Although the PVP does not stop home growers saving seeds and growing their own, there has not yet been an official source of the seeds.

I have listed the Pepperdew™ as a *Capsicum annuum*. Many descriptions speculate that it is a *C. baccatum*, but it is listed as *C. annuum* in a 1998 copy of the Australian *Plant Varieties Journal* as part of the local PVP application.

There are varieties of chilies similar to the Pepperdew™ that you could grow at home. The Malawi Piquanté, for example, looks similar in size and shape, but is listed as a *C. baccatum*. I have also come across "Pepperdew" seeds for sale on eBay and Amazon that may be genuine.

15 Pimientos de Padrón

SPECIES
....

C. annuum

SCOVILLE
RATING
....

1,000–5,000
SHU

This chili is in the top 101 not for its extreme heat, of which it provides very little, but for the way it is eaten. The Pimientos de Padrón have become part of the Spanish tapas craze that has spread around the world.

The name comes from the municipality of Padrón in northwest Spain where they are grown. It is said that they were brought back from South America in the 16th century by missionaries. So famous have these chilies become that, since 1979, they have been celebrated by holding the Festa do Pemento de Padrón each August in Herbón near Padrón.

Preparation is simple. The peppers are fried in a heavy saucepan with a little olive oil until the skin just starts to char and blister. They are then sprinkled with a little sea salt and served. Eat them just by holding the stem and biting off the fleshy chili.

They are best harvested when immature, when 1–1½ inches long. They should be bright to yellowish green with curved furrows along the skin. If left to mature, they will grow to 4 inches and turn a bright red. At this point, they will all be hot, again not searing, but at just about 3,000 Scoville heat units. So if you grow some and you are not getting any hot ones, you will need to let them mature a little longer and try again.

POD DESCRIPTION

Pods begin bright green and mature to bright red. They grow to 4 inches.

GROWING INFO

This is a fairly simple pepper to grow. It enjoys full sun, and seed germination needs 64°–72°F. The plant will grow to about 1 foot 8 inches high. With the right conditions, it will produce pods from late spring to mid-fall and even late fall, if you are lucky.

SEED SUPPLIERS

BCS, CB, CH, LS, NN, PSEU, RFC, SDCF, SLP, SSS, TCPC, TWF

USAGE

If you do forget a few and let them mature, they are great stuffed with cheese or chili con carne and baked.

16 Cascabel

SPECIES

C. annuum

SCOVILLE
RATING

1,500–2,000
SHU

Cascabel is Spanish for "rattle"—these chilies get their name because of the sound they produce after they have been dried and the loose seeds rattle about inside.

Grown commercially in Mexico, they tend to be most readily available in dried form. Make them into a paste by cutting them open and removing the seeds, then dry-frying in a saucepan. Add the dry-fried chilies to some just boiled water and let steep for 12–15 minutes before blending into a smooth paste. This paste is best used within a few days. Why not try spreading some on the skin of a chicken before roasting, or add to some olive oil and then drizzle over a salad or on to tomato soup?

POD DESCRIPTION

The fresh pods grow to about 1¼ inches in diameter in the shape of a stubby plum tomato, starting green and maturing to red. When dried, they take on a rich, dark brown.

GROWING INFO

Let these ripen to completely red before harvesting and then dry for the best flavor and color. Seeds from dried supermarket pods may not germinate, because they have been frozen and processed.

SEED SUPPLIERS

SLP

AKA

Chili Bola (Spanish for "ball chili"), Coras (when dried), Guajones (when dried), Jingle Bell, Rattle chili.

USAGE

It can be used fresh in salsa or stuffed with cream cheese. It is best to remove the seeds, because they almost fill the skin. When dried, they make an excellent powder or dried red pepper flakes, ideal for soups and casseroles.

17 Kashmiri Mirch

SPECIES
....

C. annuum

SCOVILLE
RATING
....

1,500–2,000
SHU

The Kashmiri Mirch chili is a mild chili from India that is used to impart its deep red color to Indian dishes, such as Rogan Josh, and is the Indian equivalent of Hungarian paprika (see page 36). It is also found in the spice blend deggi mirch, which is made from chilies selected to give a consistent natural color.

So popular is the Kashmiri chili that demand has outstripped supply, with fake Kashmiri powder becoming common. I have never seen the pods sold fresh but always as dried chilies or as chili powder. I like to buy them dried whole and grind them myself. You can also rehydrate them to make a paste by soaking them in warm water for 10 minutes and then using a blender or a large mortar and pestle to make a paste, which can then be stirred into your curry dishes during cooking.

Kashmiri chili seeds are available from some specialty suppliers, but I have grown them from seeds collected from the dried pods purchased in my local Indian supermarket. Although germination rates have not been especially high (you never know how old the pods are), you do get a lot of seeds this way. I have struggled to get mine to completely ripen.

POD DESCRIPTION

These pods grow to 2½–3½ inches long and 1½–2 inches wide with a gently curving body tapering to a point.

GROWING INFO

Likes the warm conditions of a greenhouse or hoop house in cool climates.

SEED SUPPLIERS

PSEU, SLP, UKCS

18 Cherry Bomb

SPECIES

C. annuum

POD DESCRIPTION

The slightly pointed, round pods ripen from dark green to red and can grow to about 2½ inches long and 1½ inches wide.

GROWING INFO

Both the Cherry Bomb F1 and the Rodeo are easy to grow and especially productive. They are early to produce pods; pick these as soon as they ripen to keep the plant productive. These plants like full sun and make ideal plants for containers. They look nice and compact and will grow to about 2 feet high.

SEED SUPPLIERS

BS, CH, LS, NN, PBPC, SS

I am not sure if the Cherry Bomb get its name from the small explosive device whose name it shares, but they can look similar. The explosive device is a small ball of resin mixed with a filler, such as sawdust, with a core of some pyrotechnic mix and a short fuse sticking out the top. The chili is a small, ball-shaped pod with a green stem sticking out the top.

Note that there is also a strain of marijuana called Cherry Bomb—you have been warned.

This is a prolific little chili plant that has become popular, because it is so simple to grow and produces such a successful crop. The Cherry Bomb is an F1 hybrid (see page 9) from U.S. specialty seed company Seminis. As an F1 variety, saving seeds will not produce the same chili, but there is now a good open-pollination alternative called the Rodeo. It is one of the easiest chilies to grow and it is slightly more upright than the Cherry Bomb.

One of the best and simplest ways to process the pods is to cut them in half and remove the seeds; they can then be frozen for later use. If you carefully cut off the top and discard the seeds, they make an excellent little chili to stuff with a cheese mix and then bake or broil.

SCOVILLE RATING

2,500–5,000 SHU

19 Guajillo

SPECIES

C. annuum

SCOVILLE
RATING

2,000–5,000
SHU

The Guajillo is the dried version of the Mirasol chili with a tough, thick skin and thin flesh. *Mirasol* means "looking at the sun," which becomes obvious when you see these chilies pointing through the leaves. With the pods growing erect, they are easily manually harvested.

After the Jalapeño (see page 60), this is one of the most popular chilies grown in Mexico. In some regions, they are used as part of the Mexican national dish Mole, the dark red/brown color of the dried pods complementing the color of the dish.

The dried Guajillo makes an excellent, but simple, thick sauce with the addition of just a few basic ingredients. First cut open 10 to 12 Guajillo pods lengthwise and remove the seeds and stems, then dry-fry the skins for a couple of minutes before soaking them in a little hot water for 20–30 minutes (reserve the water). Put the chilies and a little of the reserved water into a blender or food processor and reduce to a fine paste.

Add two or three cloves of fresh garlic and some oregano (Mexican is best here, if you are able to get hold of it). Add a little salt and continue to blend, adding a little more of the reserved water, as needed, to make a fine paste.

Make a sauce to smear on chicken as a marinade before cooking, or as a sauce on tortillas. Swirl some into baked beans for the ultimate beans on toast.

Seeds are available, but it can be easier just to buy the pods dried, because they are grown in such large numbers.

POD DESCRIPTION

The pods ripen to a dark red, are 4–5½ inches long and 1¼ –2 inches wide, and have a smooth skin and conical shape.

GROWING INFO

The plant grows to about 2 feet high; it likes moist but not wet soil, enjoys a warm, sunny position, and needs to be well-fed (sounds like me).

SEED SUPPLIERS

CH, CSB, CSU, NMSU, SLP

20

Purple Tiger

This is a stunning-looking ornamental plant with
variegated leaves of white, purple, and green,
making it a decorative container plant.

It produces plenty of pods, which start off
green before turning purple and then, finally,
red. As the color changes, the pods can take on
two colors. Green pods get dark purple stripes,
becoming lighter as the green fades and the red
appears. The red combines with the purple to
produce darker purple stripes that then fade
to a bright red.

This is one of the simplest chilies to germinate
and grow. It can be grown easily indoors or
outside on a patio.

SCOVILLE
RATING

2,000–6,000
SHU

21

Bulgarian Carrot

C. annuum

POD DESCRIPTION

The pods, which mature to a beautiful orange, grow up to 4 inches long and about 1 inch wide.

GROWING INFO

The plants grow to about 2 feet and should produce a good crop of pods. They are a great early season variety. Like most chilies, they like full sun and can be grown in large flowerpots on a sunny patio.

SEED SUPPLIERS

BPC, BS, CSB, HS, LS, NN, PZW, SDCF, SLP, SS, VNG

AKA

Shipkas

USAGE

Ideal chopped up in a salad or used to make jelly.

This heritage variety (see page 8) from Bulgaria/Hungary produces beautiful carrot-shaped pods that start off green and mature to yellow until turning orange when completely mature.

You can really appreciate the color when making delicious Bulgarian Carrot Jelly, perhaps adding raisins or golden raisins.

SCOVILLE RATING

2,000–8,000 SHU

22 Hungarian Hot Wax

SPECIES

C. annuum

POD DESCRIPTION

Banana-shaped pods
that ripen from light
yellow to red, 8 inches
long and 2 inches in
diameter.

GROWING INFO

The plants are compact
and bushy, but can reach
almost 3 feet 3 inches
high and 1 foot 8 inches
wide. Because of the
weight of the pods, they
may need support,
otherwise the branches
would probably break.

SEED SUPPLIERS

BPC, BS, CH, CSB, HS,
LS, NN, PZW, SDCF,
SLP, SS, SSS, UKCS,
VNG

Hungarian Hot Wax is one of those standard varieties that belongs in any top 10 list, let alone a top 101 list. It is a dependable variety, producing a heavy crop of banana-shaped, fleshy pods that ripen from a pale yellow to orange, then red.

They are a low to medium heat with a good flavor, making them a useful and versatile chili in the kitchen. For people who do not crave especially hot food, Hungarian Hot Wax can satisfy all their chili cooking needs, acting as a vegetable and a spice chili. This makes this variety the chili of choice for home gardeners who will be growing only one or two chili plants.

Do not be confused by the inclusion of "Hot" in the name; it does not mean the pods are especially hot, but just that they are chilies instead of sweet peppers. The term "Wax" is used to describe the glossy sheen of the skin; most of the wax-type peppers are sweet peppers, not chili peppers.

SCOVILLE
RATING

2,000–8,000
SHU

23 Bishop's Hat

SPECIES

C. baccatum

POD DESCRIPTION

The distinctive, winged pods start light lime-green and mature to a bright red. They can grow to about 2½ inches wide and long.

GROWING INFO

They like a warm 68°F outside temperature, and in cool climates these do best in a greenhouse. They can seem to take a long time to ripen.

SEED SUPPLIERS

BS, CSB, PBPC, SS

AKA

Ají Flor, Bishop's Crown, Cambuci, Campane, Christmas Bell, Friar's Hat, Joker's Hat, Monk's Hat, Pimenta Cambuci, Tinkerbell, Ubatuba Cambuci.

USAGE

Their crispness makes them ideal in a fresh salsa or sprinkled over a salad.

This three- or four-sided chili is most unusual in that it is wider than it is long. It is named Bishop's Hat or Bishop's Crown after the hat often worn by bishops, the shape of which could be said to be similar, although it may be sold as Campane in the United States. With its winged, almost flying-saucer look, it does make a good conversation piece.

The plant needs space to grow, reaching up to 6 feet 6 inches high, but can produce a good crop of 50–100 pods and is good for overwintering.

There are a number of variations on the name of this chili (see left). They may not all be the exact same variety, but I suspect they share a common heritage. A larger version of the Bishop's Hat called the Nepalese Bell is also worth growing, if you can find seeds.

SCOVILLE RATING

2,000–10,000 SHU

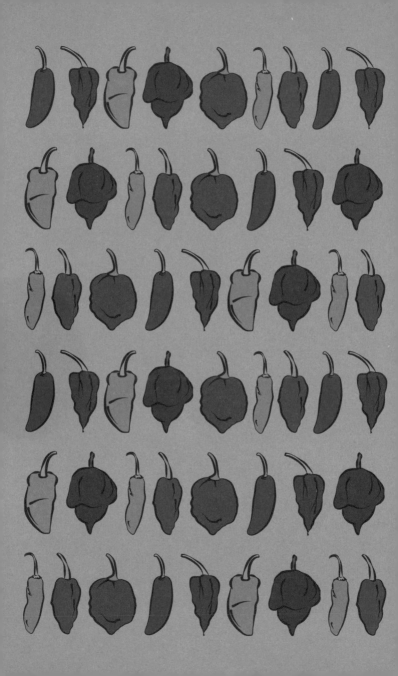

Warm

Jalapeño
Sport Pepper
Piment d'Espelette
Wenk's Yellow Hot Pepper
Chimayó
Urfa Biber
Pasilla de Oaxaca
Chipotle
NuMex Sunrise, Sunset & Eclipse
Ací Sivri Pepper
Fish Pepper
NuMex Mirasol
Aleppo Pepper
NuMex Heritage Big Jim
Serrano
De Arbol
Facing Heaven
Rocoto
Cayenne Pepper
Criolla Sella
Black Pearl
Joe's Long Cayenne
Peter Pepper
Poinsettia
Shata Baladi
Yatsafusa

Demon Red
Diavolilli
Ají Amarillo
Bangalore Torpedo
NuMex Twilight
Pusa Jwala
Sibirischer Haus Paprika
Tabasco
Dundicut
Goat Horn Pepper
Bacio di Satana
Super Chili F1 & Super Tramp
Purple Haze
Cheiro Roxa
Coffee Bean
Tepin & Pequin
Ají Cereza
Murupi Amarela
Ají Pinguita de Mono
Apache F1
Turtle Claw & Submarine
Thai Dragon
Prairie Fire
Siling Labuyo
Wiri Wiri

24 Jalapeño

C. annuum

SCOVILLE
RATING

2,500–10,000
SHU

Taking its name from the capital of the Veracruz region of Mexico, Jalapa (or Xalapa), the Jalapeño is the world's most popular chili and it seems to be everywhere. It has been included in apps and video games (as in *Plants Vs. Zombies*, where exploding Jalapeños destroy a complete row of zombies) and Texas even designated the Jalapeño its state pepper in 1995.

Generally thought of as a mild variety, there have been efforts to make Jalapeño milder by crossbreeding with the bell pepper. Known as the TAM Mild Jalapeño, or Tamed Jalapeño, and developed by Dr. Villalon at Texas A&M University, it rates at only about 1,000 SHU. This release in 1981 helped push revenue sales of salsa past those of ketchup in the United States and opened up a new market area for people who found even the Jalapeño too hot.

With its thick flesh, the Jalapeño is not easy to sun-dry, so at the end of the growing season they are left to ripen to red and then dried over the heat and smoke of large, well-controlled wood fires. The resulting dried and smoked chili is known as the Chipotle (see page 74).

The Jalapeño includes many different varieties, each with their own special characteristics. One seed catalog lists 28 varieties, each based on the original but bred to provide some specialty requirement. For instance, there are larger pods, such as the Huachinango, Jalapeño Jumbo, and the Jalapeño Goliath F1, as well as varieties with higher heat levels and early cropping varieties, such as the Centella and Tamayo.

POD DESCRIPTION

Generally bought in its green, immature state, it ripens to a dark crimson. The pods are often a bullet shape, with almost parallel sides and a rounded end. A particular characteristic (not found in supermarket versions) is "corking" of small, brown lines on the skin, considered a much sought-after sign of quality in Mexico.

GROWING INFO

Easy but requires plenty of sunlight and frequent watering. Harvest often to keep producing, but don't forget we tend to eat them when they are still immature.

SEED SUPPLIERS

BPC, BS, CCN, CH, CSB, CSU, HS, MWCH, NMSU, NN, PBPC, PJ, PN, PSEU, PZW, SDCF, SSS, TF, TWF, UKCS, VNG

USAGE

Everywhere, including on pizzas and nachos, as the flavoring for snacks, or stuffed with cream cheese as a Jalapeño Popper.

25

Sport Pepper

SPECIES

C. annuum

POD DESCRIPTION

These long slender pods will ripen to red, but are best used when green. They grow to 1½–2 inches long and ¾ inch wide.

GROWING INFO

Easy to grow and should produce a good crop. Pick the pods at the immature green stage.

SEED SUPPLIERS

MWCH, PSEU

USAGE

Pickled in vinegar.

This probably isn't a real pepper variety, but if you visit Chicago you will find jars of these everywhere—they are a traditional topping for a Chicago-style hot dog. The pods are pickled in distilled white vinegar with just a little salt.

A Chicago hot dog is a work of art in its construction. Starting with a 100 percent beef hot dog and a long, poppy seed bun, the toppings include yellow mustard, a green pepper relish, chopped sweet onions, tomato slices, a couple of pickled dill slices, at least two Sport Peppers, and then a light sprinkling of celery salt.

I would say Sport Peppers were similar to Long Thai-style pods but, having said that, it seems that I could be proved wrong, because a number of seed companies are selling seeds called Sport Pepper or Sport Chili, which they describe as like a Tabasco (see page 126) but larger.

Making your own pickled Sport Peppers could not be simpler. Take 20 to 30 thin green Thai chilies or (Sport Peppers, if you can find them). Wash them and then make a small hole in the top and near the bottom of each with a toothpick. Add them to a large stainless steel pot with 4 cups of distilled white vinegar and a couple of teaspoons of salt, bring to a boil, and simmer for 2–3 minutes. Carefully place the chilies lengthwise in a sterilized jar and pour the hot vinegar over them, seal the jar, and let cool. Once cooled, they are best stored in the refrigerator. After a couple of weeks, you will have—as near as possible—genuine Sport Peppers.

SCOVILLE RATING

2,500–10,000 SHU

26 Piment d'Espelette

SPECIES

C. annuum

POD DESCRIPTION

These can grow to 3¼–4½ inches long and 1¼–1½ inches wide with a slight curve to thick, cylindrical, red pods. When dried, they take on a darker red color.

GROWING INFO

This chili has been acclimatized to its native environment and soil conditions—a little acidic and free draining—over many years.

SEED SUPPLIERS

BPC, NMSU, SDCF, SLP, SS

AKA

Espelette Pepper, Ezpeletako Bipera, Pimient de Espelette.

SCOVILLE RATING

3,000–6,000 SHU

The Piment d'Espelette comes from the northern Basque area in France. All production takes place among the 10 villages of the Pyrénées-Atlantiques (Ainhoa, Cambo-les-Bains, Espelette, Halsou, Itxassou, Jatxou, Larressore, Saint-Pée-sur-Nivelle, Souraïde, and Ustaritz).

The story goes that the pepper was introduced to the region in 1523 by a Basque navigator, Gonzalo Percaztegi, who traveled with Christopher Columbus on his second American voyage. The Piment d'Espelette is now protected by AOC (Appellation d'Origine Contrôlée) status at the national level, and by PDO (Protected Designation of Origin) certification at the European level. The AOC covers the chilies sold as powder, on cords (like *ristras*, which are colorful strings of dried chilies) and whole and fresh in small, open boxes. Interestingly, the AOC does not cover bulk or individual pods, plants, or seeds. All of the products must be produced, transformed, and packaged within geographical boundaries specified by identified and authorized operators.

This prized pepper even has its own festival, which started in 1967. In 2018, they will be holding the fiftieth festival, which will make it the oldest chili festival in the world.

You can get seeds for this pepper and grow them at home, but, as is the case with the Chimayó chili (see page 68), a lot of what makes this pepper special is what the French call *terroir*. The unique Basque region, its climate, and growing conditions come together to make something exceptional.

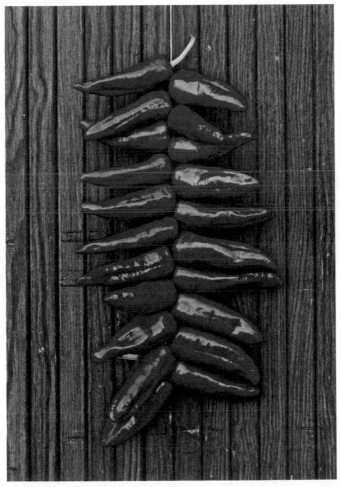

27 Wenk's Yellow Hot Pepper

SPECIES

C. annuum

POD DESCRIPTION

The pods grow to a length of 2–4 inches and are similar to a Jalapeño (see page 60) in shape, but they have a more waxy skin.

GROWING INFO

Seeds for this are more rare than might be expected for such a well-known variety. It is easy to grow and is a good producer. Pick the pods at all stages of development and keep Erris's heritage alive.

SEED SUPPLIERS

CCN, SLP, TCPC

There are some names that just seem to stand out and Erris Wenk, the developer of the Wenk's Yellow Hot Pepper, is one of those names. Little seems to be known about this farmer from Albuquerque, New Mexico, but his chili lives on in seed collections.

This chili was developed over many years to suit the growing conditions in Albuquerque. For a variety that is called Wenk's Yellow, it may seem strange that, although this chili does start out pale yellow, to reach its full potential, it will turn orange and then completely ripen to red.

You will find the Wenk's Yellow listed in the Ark of Taste (see page 9), so please grow and pass some of these on to younger generations. Isn't it time we saw a Wenk's Pickle at a local food festival?

SCOVILLE RATING

3,000–8,000 SHU

28 Chimayó

SPECIES

C. annuum

POD DESCRIPTION

The pods grow up to
12 inches long and can
be a little unpredictable
in shape, but turn from
green to red when
completely mature.

GROWING INFO

Not a hard chili to grow
or germinate, but the
seed supply may be a
little erratic.

SEED SUPPLIERS

BCS, CCN, NMSU, NN,
SLP

This is another regional specialty pepper that comes from the town of the same name Chimayó in New Mexico. This one was another that was nearly lost—or, at least, confused—because other chilies were being passed off as Chimayó.

The history of this chili possibly dates back to the 1500s, when chilies were first introduced to the area by Spanish explorers.

Just a few years ago it was being grown by just three farmers. Now, thanks to the work of a nonprofit group called The Chimayó Chili Farmers Inc., which was founded in 2005 to work with local farmers, this chili is making a comeback.

In 2005, José Alfonso and Victoria Martinez donated Chimayó seeds to the project and, by 2007, the project had been able to provide 21 new growers with seeds.

In 2006, the group worked with local farmers to apply for a trademark for Chimayó to provide legal protection and, in 2009, they were granted a registered certification mark.

Although you may be able to grow this chili at home, part of what makes it special are the conditions in which it grows in New Mexico, similar to the French *terroir* concept for grapes and wine. Here, the special characteristics—the geography, geology, and climate of Chimayó—interact with the plant genetics.

SCOVILLE
RATING

4,000–6,000
SHU

29 Urfa Biber

SPECIES
....
C. annuum

This chili comes from a region in Turkey called Şanlıurfa, where it is grown and processed. A simple explanation of the name is that in Turkish *Biber* means "pepper" and *Urfa* is the local shortened name for *Şanlıurfa*.

This is one of the few processed chilies that is probably almost impossible to re-create at home. Although seeds are available so you can grow the plants yourself, the pods are uniquely processed. They are sun-dried during the day and then wrapped tightly at night to retain the moisture. The resulting pods are then crushed to produce the dark, reddish purple flakes that you would think had been rubbed in a light oil.

POD DESCRIPTION

The fresh pods are large, at 2¾–4 inches long.

GROWING INFO

Not hard to grow, but the uniqueness of this pepper is in the way the pods are processed.

SEED SUPPLIERS

BPC, MWCH, RFC, TCPC, UKCS

USAGE

Try adding some flakes to roasted vegetables or when making a soup. The flakes are also good sprinkled on scrambled eggs and you can add the flakes to a bottle of olive oil and let infuse for homemade chili oil. The fresh pods are ideal sliced and added to a salad.

SCOVILLE RATING

4,000–9,000 SHU

Pasilla de Oaxaca

SPECIES

C. annuum

POD DESCRIPTION

You will find these dried and sold in packs. These chilies are 4–5½ inches long and 1½ inches wide, tapering to ¾–1¼ inches at the base.

GROWING INFO

Some seeds are available, but there is a lot of confusion over what is the fresh variety that produces the Pasilla de Oaxaca; it may be that there is no single variety that is the true Pasilla de Oaxaca. Whichever variety you select to grow, remember that these expect a warm environment and plenty of sun.

SEED SUPPLIERS

NMSU

SCOVILLE
RATING

4,000–10,000
SHU

This is a smoke-dried chili from the Mixe region in the state of Oaxaca in Mexico. Oaxaca is famous for the range of chilies it produces, including the Chilhuacle Nego, Chilhuacle Roja, and Chilhuacle Amarillo, but the rarest of them all is the Pasilla de Oaxaca.

There is some confusion, because the Poblano and its dried forms, the Ancho and Mulato (see page 34), are often called Pasilla in southern California, although the more common Pasilla mentioned in recipes and found in specialty stores is a long, thin, dried Chilaca chili.

It may be that the true fresh version of the Pasilla de Oaxaca is the Chili de Agua, which translates as "water chili." This 4–5½-inch-long by ¾–1¼-inch-wide chili is grown in small quantities, and it is rumored that this was the chili that was used to create the original Chili Relleno (see page 33), which is now made almost exclusively with Poblano chilies.

Pasilla de Oaxaca is one of the chilies I would most like to try fresh. With so few being grown and even fewer smoked and dried, I have tried for years to get hold of some fresh pods. This chili should probably be included in the Slow Food Foundation Ark of Taste (see page 9) before it completely disappears.

Smoked chilies have become a sensation in the past few years, with the Chipotle (see page 74) becoming the flavor of choice for adding to almost anything. Maybe the Pasilla de Oaxaca could have such a future.

31 Chipotle

SPECIES
....
C. annuum

SCOVILLE
RATING
....
5,000–10,000
SHU

This is the chili that seems to be added to almost everything these days, and it is not even a real chili variety. *Chipotle* comes from the Nahuatl (Aztec) language and basically means "smoked chili pepper."

The Chipotle is a smoked Jalapeño chili (see page 60). The Jalapeño is normally eaten when green, but at the end of the growing season it is left to turn red, and the mature Jalapeños are then smoked to preserve them.

There are two main types of Chipotle: the Meco and the Morita. The Morita is smaller than the Meco and is smoked for less time. It has a dark red exterior and is generally the cheaper of the two. The Meco, although larger, also has a smoked, dusty look to it and, of the two, has a much more smoky and robust flavor.

There is also the Chipotle Grande, which is a smoke-dried Huachinango chili. This is a Jalapeño-type chili, but, at 4–6 inches long, it is much larger.

To make things even more confusing, there is also the Jalapeño Chico, which is a Jalapeño that is green when it is smoked.

POD DESCRIPTION

The size depends on the Jalapeño variety used, but the Chipotle Grande pods can grow up to 6 inches long.

GROWING INFO

Start by growing Jalapeños (see page 60).

SEED SUPPLIERS

See Jalapeños (page 60)

AKA

Chili Ahumado, Chili Meco, Chili Morita, Chili Navideño, Chili Típico.

32 NuMex Sunrise, Sunset & Eclipse

SPECIES

C. annuum

POD DESCRIPTION

The NuMex Sunrise turns a bright yellow, the NuMex Sunset is orange, and the NuMex Eclipse turns a deep brown. The pods are all the same shape and size, at 4–6 inches long and ¾–1¼ inches wide, with thin flesh, which is ideal for drying.

GROWING INFO

The plants like a sunny position and grow to about 2 feet high and 17½ inches wide, so they can be planted in large containers as patio plants.

SEED SUPPLIERS

BPC, CSB, MWCH, NMSU, SLP

USAGE

Ornamentals that are also ideal for drying for dried pepper flakes and also good when pickled whole.

These three chilies, developed at the New Mexico Agricultural Experiment Station by Paul W. Bosland, Jaime Iglesias, and Steve D. Tanksley, were all developed from the same parents and are a cross between the Permagreen bell pepper and the New Mexico 6–4 (which produces pods that are 4¼–8 inches long).

They were grown as ornamentals for use in colorful chili *ristras* (strings of chilies), which are particularly popular in New Mexico and as souvenirs for tourists. Don't be put off by the ornamental tag, because these three can also be used in cooking. They make the most interesting pickled chilies when combined whole in jars (do make sure to prick some holes in the pods with a toothpick before pickling to let the pickling mix enter the chilies). Once dried, you can crush them to make tricolored pepper flakes.

SCOVILLE RATING

3,000–5,000 SHU

33

Ac í Sivri Pepper

SPECIES

C. annuum

SCOVILLE
RATING

5,000–30,000
SHU

The Ací Sivri Pepper is of Turkish origin. It is a Cayenne-style chili pepper (see page 96) and produces long, slender pods; they tend to curl a little as they grow.

The pods mature to a deep red but start as a yellowish green; the longer they mature, the hotter they get. If you still have a lot of green pods at the end of the season, an excellent tip is to seed and then pickle them in vinegar with a few spices.

This pepper is often listed as an heirloom variety (see page 8). It grows up to 3 feet high and is a good producer of pods, with as many as 50 per plant.

POD DESCRIPTION

Long, slender pods growing to 8½ inches long and ½–¾ inch wide. Pods start a yellow-green and mature to dark red.

GROWING INFO

Will need some space, because they grow to 3 feet high and will need support when completely matured.

SEED SUPPLIERS

BS, PBPC, SLP

USAGE

Being thin fleshed, they dry well, but they are also excellent pickled when green.

34 Fish Pepper

SPECIES

C. annuum

POD DESCRIPTION

The pods begin almost white, then become green with variegated white streaks, then turn orange and brown and, finally, the whole pod turns red. They grow to 1¼–2 inches long and ½–¾ inch wide, and have a blunt, rounded tip.

GROWING INFO

They will grow well to about 2 feet high in gardener's grow bags filled with seed and potting mix and in a greenhouse. However, they will need support, because the limited room in the soil mix does not give much support to the root system.

SEED SUPPLIERS

BPC, CH, CSB, HS, LS, SLP, VNG

This African-American heirloom variety (see page 8) is believed to have started as a natural mutation of the Serrano pepper (see page 88).

The pods start almost white, before becoming green with variegated white streaks that develop to orange and brown. Finally, the whole pod turns red when completely mature. Not only the pods, but also the leaves and the stems of the pods are variegated, making this an attractive plant. It can be easily grown in containers, because the plants are compact and grow to about 2 feet high.

Why this chili mutation has survived is probably due to the fact that in its immature state, when it is almost white, it can be added to a white sauce or a chowder as a hidden heat.

Remember, although the pod looks most interesting in the variegated white and green stage, any saved seeds will only be viable once the pods have completely matured to red.

Seeds are becoming commercially available, but they were almost unheard of just a few years ago outside the Philadelphia/Baltimore region of the country.

SCOVILLE RATING

5,000–30,000 SHU

35 NuMex Mirasol

SPECIES

C. annuum

POD DESCRIPTION

The pods start green and ripen to a bright red and, at 2 inches long and ¾ inch wide, they make a great display.

GROWING INFO

This is a good compromise chili plant when you have little space and need something that not only looks good but can be used as well.

SEED SUPPLIERS

CCN, MWCH, PSEU, SLP, TCPC

USAGE

Although considered an ornamental chili, with the plants being small and bushy, they are an especially usable chili in cooking and are ideal for making into flakes or chili powders.

This is a chili where the pods point upward, hence *Mirasol*, which is Spanish for "looking at the sun." This variety was developed at the New Mexico Agricultural Experiment Station by Paul W. Bosland and Max M. Gonzalez and released in 1993–94 to fit a special niche in the market for a chili plant that could be used to create decorative chili wreathes (*ristras*) and for flower arranging. Ristras need to have leaves and pods together to create a good contrast. This plant produces clusters of long, thin-fleshed, conical pods that dry well and retain their color.

This variety was developed by crossing the Santaka chili and the La Blanca and then stabilizing the variety over seven generations.

SCOVILLE RATING

5,000–30,000 SHU

36 Aleppo Pepper

C. annuum

POD DESCRIPTION

The pods ripen to dark
red and grow up to
about 4 inches long
and ¾–1¼ inches wide,
slightly tapering to a
blunt end.

GROWING INFO

A good, sturdy plant, but
it will need support and
space to grow.

SEED SUPPLIERS

BPC, CCN, PBPC

AKA

Halab Pepper (*Halab*
is the Arabic name
for "Aleppo"), Halaby
Pepper.

USAGE

Usually sold sun-dried,
crushed and mixed with
salt and olive oil.

SCOVILLE
RATING

8,000–12,000
SHU

The Aleppo Pepper is named after the city of
Aleppo in northern Syria. Aleppo is the largest
city in Syria and had a population of more than 2
million. It was once known for being on the Silk
Road, which extended 4,000 miles from China to
the edge of Europe.

Traditionally, this pepper is sun-dried, seeded,
crushed, and mixed with salt and olive oil, and
it is in this form that it is mostly available from
specialty retailers. It is a good pantry staple for
when things need a lift and is a great flavoring for
soups and stuffing mixes.

Seeds are becoming available, so you can grow
this pepper at home.

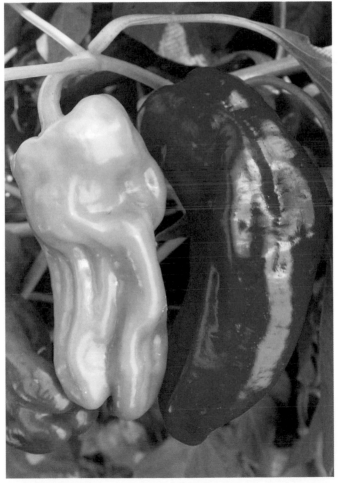

37 NuMex Heritage Big Jim

SPECIES

C. annuum

POD DESCRIPTION

Pods have thick flesh and are 6–8 inches in length.

GROWING INFO

I had great success with these a few years ago by setting the propagator to 64–68°F; they like daytime temperatures above 63°F and the seeds sprouted within a few days. The plants can grow to 3 feet 3 inches high and 1 foot 8 inches in width, so they will need some space to grow.

SEED SUPPLIERS

BS, CH, CSB, CSU, LS, NN, NMSU, PBPC, PZW, SDCF, SLP, VNG

SCOVILLE RATING

7,000–9,000 SHU

The original NuMex Big Jim is listed in *The Guinness Book of Records* as having the world's largest chili pods at 13½ inches, but over the years this New Mexican-style chili was starting to show losses in yield and heat as well as other significant growing characteristics.

So the New Mexico State University Chili Pepper Breeding and Genetics Program set about returning this variety to its original specification, if not improving it a little. This process took almost 10 years from obtaining a 200-seed sample from the Plant Germplasm Preservation Research Unit, where the original seeds had been preserved, to 2007, when they had established a new superior chili, which was released as the NuMex Heritage Big Jim.

The process involved growing plants for seeds in controlled, insect-free conditions and then selecting just the plants that met the required criteria, doing this again and again, increasing the number of plants and those selected, until a stable variety was produced.

This new chili variety maintained the virtues that made the original Big Jim so popular, but was much better suited to commercial growing, being more uniform in the plant's height and width and its maturity date.

The new Big Jim produces an increased yield of about 11 percent on average. The heat has increased to 9,000 SHU while retaining the required flavor profile.

38 Serrano

SPECIES
....
C. annuum

SCOVILLE
RATING
....
10,000–30,000
SHU

These little, bullet-shape chilies are one of my favorites. They have a thin skin but thick, crunchy flesh, making them great chilies to use in a fresh salsa. I like to roast some ripe red ones on the barbeque grill before I start cooking the meat, then finely chop them and add them to my tomato salsa.

The Serrano originates from the Sierra mountains of Mexico, and its name is from *sierras*, meaning "mountains." The plants can grow to 2¼–3 feet high.

If you have a lot of green Serranos, use them to make a simple salsa verde. Remove the stems from 10 to 20 green Serranos, coarsely chop 5 or 6 green tomatoes, a large bunch of fresh cilantro, and a large, mild onion, and add them to a blender or food processor with 2 garlic cloves. Process to an almost liquid consistency, adding a little salt to taste, if needed. Do feel free to adapt the recipe. I use green tomatoes because I always seem to have some about at that time of year, but for a real authentic salsa verde you would use tomatillos.

There are a number of interesting varieties of Serrano, including the Serrano Tampiqueno, which produces much larger pods, and the faster-maturing and milder F1 hybrid (see page 9), the Serrano del Sol, which is my favorite to grow.

POD DESCRIPTION

These pods grow to 2–2¾ inches long and ¾–1¼ inches in diameter.

GROWING INFO

The plants can be grown in large containers. Oddly, I have found these grow better when you keep a few of them together. They will produce more than 50 pods, if you get the conditions right.

SEED SUPPLIERS

BCS, CB, CF, CH, HS, LS, MWCH, NMSU, NN, PSEU, PZW, RFC, SDCF, SLP, SS, TCPC, TF, TWF, VNG

39 De Arbol

SPECIES
....

C. annuum

SCOVILLE
RATING
....

15,000–30,000
SHU

These long, slender chilies from Mexico can grow to up to 4 inches long. They look much like the Cayenne varieties (see page 96) but the flavor is different. The De Arbol has a more nutty, smoky flavor without the peppery hints of a Cayenne and you will see the De Arbol listed in many seed catalogs as a heritage or a heirloom variety (see page 8).

De Arbol means "treelike" in Spanish, which describes the way the plant grows, because it can easily reach 4 feet high and has long, branchlike stems.

I find this chili is at its best after it has been dried, which helps to intensify the flavor. Once they are dried, the pods can be seeded and ground to make a powder or flakes. If you are using them whole, open them up, remove the seeds, and then lightly dry-fry them to help release the oils and aroma.

Most chilies darken when dehydrated and some thin-skinned varieties become semitranslucent. The De Arbol, in contrast, seems to retain its bright red color. When buying dried, always choose the brightest-looking chilies, because they darken with age.

POD DESCRIPTION

These are long, slender, thin-fleshed chilies that can have small undulations or constrictions in the flesh. They grow to 2–2¾ inches long and ¼–½ inch wide. When completely ripe, they are a deep red with smooth, shiny skin.

GROWING INFO

It can take a while for the seeds to germinate. It is a bushy plant that requires some support, because it can produce a heavy crop. It likes a position in full sun.

SEED SUPPLIERS

BPC, BS, HS, LS, NMSU, SLP

AKA

Bird's Beak chili (Pico de Pajaro) and the Rat's Tail chili (Cola de Rata), because of the long, slender shape of the pods.

USAGE

Dry and grind to make powder or flakes or lightly dry-fry whole.

40 Facing Heaven

SPECIES
....
C. annuum

SCOVILLE
RATING
....

15,000–30,000
SHU

The Facing Heaven chili gets its name from the way the pods point upward. They have become well-known through their use in Sichuan cuisine, where they are used whole in great quantities to add flavor to dishes, but you are not expected to eat the chilies unless you want to.

The pods start off green and turn bright red, making this a most ornamental-looking plant. There are a number of varieties, from long, slender pods to round, cone-shaped ones. My favorites are the cone-shaped ones, because they have a strong lemony citrus flavor and vibrant red color.

The dried pods are most often used whole at the start of cooking, dry-fried or fried in a little oil to release their flavor. One of my favorite dishes using these chilies is Sichuan hot pot, which includes fresh ginger, Sichuan pepper, and Facing Heaven chilies.

POD DESCRIPTION

The pods start off green and turn red, vary in shape, depending on the variety, are thin skinned; they grow to 1¼–2½ inches long and ½–¾ inch in diameter.

GROWING INFO

A short, bushy plant that produces a lot of pods. I saved seeds from pods purchased in an Asian supermarket, but very few germinated.

SEED SUPPLIERS

BS, CH, LS

AKA

Chao Tian Jiao, Heaven Chili, Liuzhou.

USAGE

The pods are easy to dehydrate at home, using a dehydrator, and they are also good for making chili oil.

41 Rocoto

SPECIES

C. pubescens

SCOVILLE
RATING

15,000–30,000
SHU

The Rocoto, aka Manzano, comes from a species of chilies called *Capsicum pubescens* (see page 7).

Although counted as a domesticated variety, it is one of the rarest, coming from Peru in western South America, where it is able to grow in cooler climatic conditions than most chilies. Unfortunately, it is still not frost resistant. It can be grown for a number of years, with the plant becoming almost a small chili tree in appearance.

Its other name Manzano means "apple," and these pods do look like small, round apples. They have thick flesh and skin, making them hard to dehydrate, so they are normally used fresh.

Somewhat of an oddity is the Rocoto San Isidro, which is linked to the small village of San Isidro, where it is said to be grown by a priest in the grounds of the church. San Isidro is on the island of La Palma in the Canary Islands. This is a long way from the forests of Peru and how it got there is unknown.

POD DESCRIPTION

Small, round pods grow up to 2 inches in diameter. The pods can be a little elongated, like a plum tomato. They are available in a range of colors, including red, green, orange, and yellow.

GROWING INFO

These can be a little harder to grow and do not like direct sunlight, but prefer the shade of other plants. In particularly warm summers in cool, temperate areas, as well as in warm climates, they will easily grow outside in large containers, but they will need support, because they can reach up to 6½ feet high.

SEED SUPPLIERS

BPC, CCN, CF, CH, MWCH, NN, PSEU, RFC, SLP, TF

USAGE

Use fresh to make a great, fruity base for a salsa or relish. With their round shape and thick flesh, they would also be good with the stem and seeds removed and then pickled or stuffed and roasted, such as in the Peruvian dish Rocoto Relleno.

42 Cayenne Pepper

SPECIES
....

C. annuum,
C. frutescens

SCOVILLE
RATING
....

15,000–50,000
SHU

The Cayenne pepper gets its name from the city of Cayenne in French Guiana. It is an extremely popular pepper and all supermarkets and grocers will have some form of it on sale.

It has also become synonymous with the medical uses of peppers. Cayenne has been recommended for everything from coughs, ulcers, and sore throats to the prevention of heart attacks and strokes. Some research has shown it can dissolve fibrin, a protein used in the formation of blood clots, and it may also stop plaque forming on the walls of arteries.

The diet industry has also started to catch on to its magical properties. It has been used as an appetite suppressor and is thought to help with weight loss because it raises body temperature, which, in turn, burns more energy and speeds up metabolism.

Cayenne is not a single variety of chili pepper, but a collection of chili varieties that share a common style and flavor. I have seen it described as both *Capsicum frutescens* and *C. annuum*, but most seed catalogs come down on the *C. annuum* side.

POD DESCRIPTION

A long, slender pod that starts green and ripens to red. It can grow to 12 inches long, as in the case of Joe's Long Cayenne (see page 102), but most pods are much shorter: 2–4½ inches. They do not usually exceed ½ inch wide and all taper to a sharp point.

GROWING INFO

To germinate seeds, set your propagator to 68°F and they should sprout in 5 to 10 days. Cayenne plants like space for their roots, but will grow well in larger flowerpots.

SEED SUPPLIERS

BPC, BS, CF, CH, CSB, HS, NN, PZW, SLP, SS, UKCS, VNG

AKA

African Pepper, Bird Pepper, Cockspur Pepper, Cow Horn Pepper, Devil's Tongue, Goat's Pepper, Guinea Pepper, Hot Flame, Red Bird Pepper.

USAGE

It is claimed to have medical and weight-reduction benefits, as well as culinary uses.

43

Criolla Sella

SPECIES

C. baccatum

POD DESCRIPTION

The pods start green and mature to a golden orange, 1½–2½ inches in length and ½–¾ of an inch wide, with a slender, cylindrical shape.

GROWING INFO

There are no real problems growing the Criolla Sella. It is known for being one of the best to overwinter but is not frost resistant, so in cool, temperate climates, bring inside before it gets too cold.

SEED SUPPLIERS

BPC, CCN, PBPC, SLP

USAGE

Eat as they are, freshly picked, use to make salsa or a sauce, or dry to make chili powder.

This is a great little plant from Bolivia in South America that is short, strong, and sturdy—and it needs to be, because it is generally heavily covered in pods. A great plus for this variety is that it matures early and is suited to cool, temperate climates. Being compact, it can be grown in large containers in a sun room or greenhouse and moved outside once the weather is warmer.

The Wiltshire Chilli Farm in Great Britain used them to make a single-variety sauce that really showed off this chili's unique flavor. To make the sauce, it was combined with apple cider vinegar, orange juice, and just a few spices.

Criolla Sella chilies have a delightful citrus flavor and are mild enough to be munched on straight from the plant or, my favorite, sliced and added to a cheese sandwich.

The thin skins make them ideal for drying, because they make an excellent, slightly sweet chili powder, but they also work well fresh in a salsa or sauce.

SCOVILLE HEAT UNITS

20,000–30,000 SHU

44 Black Pearl

SPECIES

C. annuum

POD DESCRIPTION

Round pods, ½–1 inch in diameter. Dark purple pods ripen to red.

GROWING INFO

These like the sun, and they are great when grown in large flowerpots on the patio.

SEED SUPPLIERS

CF, CH, HS, NN, SLP, UKCS

USAGE

Generally grown as an ornamental.

This chili is described as an ornamental and is a great-looking plant, but don't let the word "ornamental" put you off, because all peppers are edible. It has dark, almost black, leaves and bunches of round pods (black pearls) that poke upright through the foliage, and that uniquely start as dark purple and finally ripen to red.

Black Pearl has nothing to do with pirate movies. It was developed by plant geneticist John Stommel (Agricultural Research Service Vegetable Laboratory) and Robert Griesbach (Agricultural Research Service Floral & Nursery Plant Research Unit), in conjunction with PanAmerican Seeds and McCorkle Nurseries. Released in 2005, it was a winner of an All-American Selections award, recognizing its improved qualities, in 2006.

It is an ideal pepper for planting in large containers on a patio, because it only grows to 1 foot 8 inches high and 1 foot 4 inches wide, and, as peppers go, it has the looks to die for.

SCOVILLE
RATING

25,000–30,000
SHU

45

Joe's Long Cayenne

SPECIES

C. annuum

POD DESCRIPTION

Long pods, often more than 12 inches in length.

GROWING INFO

A productive and fun chili to grow, it will need support as it develops, because of the weight of the pods.

SEED SUPPLIERS

BPC, CH, NN, PJ, PSEU, PZW, SS, SSS, VNG

AKA

Pinocchio's Nose, Whippet's Tail.

USAGE

Ideal for drying.

SCOVILLE RATING

20,000–50,000 SHU

Cayenne chilies normally produce long, thin pods that taper to a point with thin flesh, but the Joe's Long Cayenne does have an extreme talent for producing long pods, the length often exceeding 12 inches.

I have been told by seed companies how easily chili varieties can multiply. This chili is a case in point. In the early 1990s, Peppers by Post, a British mail-order fresh chili business, wanted to offer a cayenne with a difference, so it looked at American seed companies and discovered Joe's Long Cayenne. As the variety was unknown in Great Britain at that time, and they did not want to give their secret variety away, they called the pods they were selling Whippet's Tail.

They never changed the name of the variety because they were selling it as a pod and not as seed, and it was deemed acceptable practice. However, within a few years, they started seeing Whippet's Tail seeds being offered for sale, and you can still see them on the Internet today.

At this time, they worked with Tozers Seed Company and showed the Joe's Long Cayenne plants to them. Tozers purchased some seeds and, in turn, offered seeds to Thompson & Morgan seed company for retail sales. However, for their retail packs, Thompson & Morgan called the seeds Pinocchio's Nose, and this was how one chili became three.

At a recent chili display at West Dean Gardens, near Chichester, Great Britain, there were three identical plants. They were labeled: Joe's Long Cayenne, Whippet's Tail, and Pinocchio's Nose.

46 Peter Pepper

SPECIES

C. annuum

POD DESCRIPTION

The pods grow to
3–4 inches long and
¾–1¼ inches wide and
ripen from green to
red. Other colors are
becoming available,
with both yellow and
orange varieties listed
in some of the online
seed catalogs.

GROWING INFO

Easy to grow in a
gardener's grow bag.
In cool, temperate
climates, the plants like
to be in a greenhouse or
sun room.

SEED SUPPLIERS

BPC, CF, HS, LS,
MWCH, NN, PJ, PSEU,
RFC, SLP, TCPC, TF,
TWF, VNG

AKA

Chilli Willy, Penis
Pepper.

USAGE

Mainly an ornamental,
although also grown on
a commercial basis for
use in hot sauces. Use in
fresh salsas.

Are these the peppers Peter Piper picked?
Probably not. The Peter Pepper had to be included
for its alternate names, Penis Pepper or Chilli
Willy. As you can probably see from the picture,
these have an unusual phallic shape that, when
ripe, resembles the human penis.

Originating from Louisiana and Texas, this
pepper is now most commonly grown as an
ornamental, because of the shape of the pod,
but it has also been grown on a limited scale
commercially for use in hot sauces.

Described as an heirloom variety (see page 8),
this pepper has only survived because it has some
culinary use. Luckily, it does taste pretty good.
Just think of the recipes you can make and name
inappropriately using this chili.

For Peter's penis pepper salsa—a simple, fresh
salsa—coarsely chop 3 or 4 ripe tomatoes and add
to a blender or food processor with 2 or 3 peeled
and chopped garlic cloves, 1 chopped onion, and
3 or 4 chopped fresh Peter Peppers. Blend to a
smooth consistency. Pour the mixture into a bowl
and add 3 or 4 chopped ripe tomatoes (to give your
salsa a chunkier texture), 3 tablespoons chopped
fresh cilantro, and lime juice to taste. Season with
salt and black pepper, mix thoroughly, and serve
with tortilla chips.

SCOVILLE RATING

25,000–35,000
SHU

47 Poinsettia

SPECIES

C. annuum

POD DESCRIPTION

The pods ripen from light green to bright red, are about 2¾ inches long and ½ of an inch wide, and taper to a point.

GROWING INFO

A beautiful-looking plant and easy to grow. If you keep it confined in a flowerpot, you can keep it on a windowsill or else it can grow to 2 feet high. A good plant for the patio or conservatory.

SEED SUPPLIERS

BS, CCN, PSEU, SLP, TWF, UKCS

AKA

Japanese Hot Claw.

USAGE

Normally grown as an ornamental, but the pods can be dried to make red pepper flakes.

With its mass of dark green leaves and clusters of bright red chili pods pointing up, the Poinsettia chili has a striking resemblance to the well-known Poinsettia plant.

Normally grown as an ornamental, this chili does produce a mass of pods that are particularly useful in the kitchen. They are best used with the seeds removed, because there are a lot of them for a pod of this size.

Poinsettia is similar to, and maybe the same as, the Takanotsume chili from Japan, which is also known as the Hawk's Claw Pepper because of its curved, talonlike shape. The Takanotsume and the Yatsufusa chilies (see page 110) are often dried and used as the main ingredients of Shichimi tōgarashi.

Poinsettias are also ideal for drying and using to make red pepper flakes. Chop off the stem and calyx, halve the pods lengthwise, and put them into a dehydrator.

SCOVILLE RATING

25,000–40,000 SHU

48 Shata Baladi

POD DESCRIPTION

The skyward-pointing, erect, green pods droop down as they enlarge and ripen from green to black/purple and then a bright red. They can grow to 1½–2¾ inches long and ¾–1¼ inches wide and can have an almost plum-tomato shape.

GROWING INFO

It is a beautiful-looking, bushy plant that can grow to 2 feet 3 inches high. It can be grown in large flowerpots or containers, but will need some warmth and sun to get the maximum out of the plants.

SEED SUPPLIERS

SLP

USAGE

Generally grown as an ornamental.

From Egypt comes the Shata Baladi, which produces a multitude of pods. With thick skins and a slightly sweet and fruity flavor, these chilies are excellent dried and ground into a mild to warm paprika. The pods have thick flesh, so you will probably need to use a dehydrator, however, it will be worth the effort, because they retain their color well. If you will be making a powder or flakes, cut the pods in half from top to bottom to aid the drying. The aroma as they dry is wonderful.

The seeds of this variety are not the easiest to find, but a search of some of the chili-growing forums should find some seeds if you cannot source any from chili seed specialty suppliers.

SCOVILLE RATING

25,000–50,000
SHU

49 Yatsafusa

SPECIES

C. annuum

POD DESCRIPTION

Long, slender pods grow upright in clusters of 5 to 6 pods from the top of each branch.

GROWING INFO

A beautiful-looking, compact plant, ideal for large flowerpots on a sunny patio.

SEED SUPPLIERS

NMSU, PBPC, PJ, PSEU

AKA

Hontaka, Japones, Santaka.

USAGE

Like other Cayenne-style peppers, it is a good variety to dehydrate, which can mean you have a source of heat and flavor all year around. When dried, it is a main ingredient of Shichimi tōgarashi.

SCOVILLE RATING

25,000–75,000 SHU

This is the Japanese equivalent of the Cayenne (see page 96), but it is better known in the West as the Japones.

This beautiful plant is a small, compact variety. *Yatsafusa*, when referring to trees, means "dwarf," and this chili grows to only 1 foot 6 inches–2 feet high, making it ideal for growing in flowerpots on a balcony or other confined space.

Yatsafusa is a key part of Sichuan cuisine and you can easily make a Sichuan-style chili oil using last year's dried pods. Finely chop 8 to 10 dried pods and put them into a heatproof glass container. In a small skillet, heat about 1 cup of oil (not olive oil in this case, because you will need an oil that can take the heat) until it starts to smoke. Remove from the heat, let it cool for a minute or two, and then carefully pour it over the chopped chilies. Cover and let cool and, once cooled, strain out the chilies.

Both the Yatsufusa and the Takanotsume chilies are dried and used as the main ingredients of Shichimi tōgarashi, a blend of spices and seasoning that is used as a table condiment for soups and noodles.

50 Demon Red

C. annuum

POD DESCRIPTION

Smooth-skinned pods grow to ¾–1½ inches long and up to a ¼ inch wide and ripen from green to red.

GROWING INFO

Easy to grow, they will reach a maximum of about 14 inches around. Grow in a smallish flowerpot and leave it out on the patio during hot summer days. This variety is not tolerant of colder climates, but it still grows indoors in a sunny position.

SEED SUPPLIERS

BS, NN, SLP, TCPC, VNG

This small, compact, ornamental chili has been bred to grow in small containers and is great for the windowsill. It produces a mass of upward-facing small pods that start green and ripen to a fiery red.

Although described as ornamental, these little pods, ¾–1½ inches long and up to a ¼ inch wide, are edible and ideally suited to Thai cooking. Like many ornamentals, these can taste a little bitter, but they have a pleasant Cayenne-style peppery flavor (see page 96).

A past winner of a British Royal Horticultural Society Award of Garden Merit, they are easy to grow. Pick them directly from the plant as you need them, but once the weather starts to cool down, pick your remaining pods and let them dry. Because they are thin fleshed, they will dry easily and keep you warm until the next season's crop is ready.

SCOVILLE RATING

30,000–50,000 SHU

51 Diavolilli

SPECIES

C. annuum

POD DESCRIPTION

Ripens from dark green to bright red, reaching 1½ inches long and a ¼ inch wide.

GROWING INFO

Nice, compact plant that is easily grown, but it will probably need a greenhouse in cool, temperate areas if it is to reach its full potential.

SEED SUPPLIERS

No commercial seed supplier has been found, so you may have to search seed exchange websites and forums.

AKA

In Italy, they are also known as Diavolicchio (Little Devil) chili or Pellegrino (Pilgrim) chili.

USAGE

Try finely sliced and fried in a little olive oil, then tossed through fresh pasta.

This is a compact, bushlike chili plant that grows to 1 foot 8 inches high and the same wide, with the pods pointing up through the foliage.

The Diavolilli chili originates from Calabria/Basilicata in southern Italy, where it is the chili used in the chili-eating competition at the Annual Diamante Peperoncino Festival. The competition entails eating as many 2-ounce plates of the chilies as possible in 30 minutes.

Sometimes you can find this variety powdered or dried in specialty stores.

SCOVILLE RATING

30,000–50,000 SHU

52 Ají Amarillo

SPECIES
....
C. baccatum

SCOVILLE
RATING
....
30,000–50,000
SHU

Amarillo translates to "yellow" and *ají* means "chili" in Spanish. This chili starts green and ripens to a deep orange and its thick flesh has a fruity flavor.

Outside of Peru and Bolivia, they can be found dried whole or as powder, when they can also be called Ají Mirasol or Cusqueno. If you buy them dried, they can be rehydrated in a little warm water for 15–20 minutes, whereas the powdered form is often used to flavor or color rice.

Ají Amarillos are a staple of Peruvian cuisine and versatile. Try rehydrating them, then blend to a fine paste and use to flavor homemade mayonnaise. If you are more adventurous, then a quick search of the Internet will find recipes, such as Causa Rellena (a potato and chicken salad), Papas a la Huancaína (potato in a white cheese sauce), and Ají de Gallina (chicken in a spicy cream sauce).

POD DESCRIPTION

Pods start green and ripen to deep orange and grow to 4–6 inches long.

GROWING INFO

Plants can grow to well over 3 feet 3 inches high. To germinate the seeds, they need a temperature above 64°F. The plants enjoy full sun but need to be kept watered, and in cool, temperate climates, they will easily grow in a sunny greenhouse or sun room.

SEED SUPPLIERS

CH, HS, LS, NN, SLP

AKA

Ají Escabeche, Ají Mirasol (dried), Cusqueno (dried), Peruvian chili.

USAGE

There are a number of commercial sauces available that are made with this chili.

53 Bangalore Torpedo

C. frutescens

POD DESCRIPTION

The pods grow to about 5 inches long and ½ an inch wide, maturing from light green to bright red.

GROWING INFO

You will need some space, because the plants tend to spread out unless trained.

SEED SUPPLIERS

HS, SS

USAGE

The pods are ideal for pickling while green, when they are milder, and for drying when mature. This chili is great for clearing sinuses.

The 10-foot-long Bangalore Torpedo developed in 1912 by the British Indian Army was used to clear mines. Unfortunately, this was not a chili plant. The plant is a long, slender Cayenne-style chili (see page 96) and is used in Indian cuisine.

This Indian chili matures from a light green to a bright red and can tend to curve and twist a little. The plant grows to 3 feet 3 inches high.

These are great pickled. You will want to wash the chilies well and prick a few holes in the flesh to let the pickling liquid do its work. Pack as many as you can into a tall, sterilized jar so you can later pull out individual chilies, and then make the pickling liquid with 2 cups of water, 2 cups of distilled white vinegar, and 2 teaspoons of noniodized salt.

Put all the ingredients into a saucepan and bring to a boil. Let cool for 10–15 minutes and then pour slowly into the jar of chilies until they are all covered, carefully tapping the jar to release any air bubbles.

Seal the jar with a tight lid and the pickled chilies should be ready to eat in a couple of weeks. They will keep, unopened, for up to a year. Once opened, store in the refrigerator.

SCOVILLE RATING

30,000–50,000 SHU

54 NuMex Twilight

This may be the ultimate chili plant for a flowerpot, because it is one of the prettiest. With the upright fruit starting purple, then ripening to yellow, orange, and red, the pods provide a more colorful display than any flowering plant. The fruiting season starts in early summer and continues right up to early winter, giving a beautiful display for a long time.

The seed is a good germinator and the plants grow easily, so, along with Super Chili F1 and Super Tramp (see page 134), NuMex Twilight is one of the easiest chili varieties to grow and suitable for beginners to try.

An alternative is a variety called Fairy Lights, which is best described as a cousin of the NuMex Twilight, except that its stems are dark purple, the leaves have an attractive purpling over them, and the flowers are completely purple.

You may well find either of these being sold by your local garden nursery, because they are both popular varieties.

SCOVILLE RATING

30,000–50,000 SHU

55 Pusa Jwala

SPECIES

C. annuum

POD DESCRIPTION

The pods will grow to 3¼–5½ inches long and ripen from light green to orange and finally red.

GROWING INFO

Designed for commercial growing, this variety needs space to develop. It is not hard to grow, but its size means it is not recommended for the home grower. If you do want to try them, I have found it best to soak the seeds for a few days before placing them in a warm place or at 68°F in a seed propagator. In cool, temperate climates, they will need a large hoop house.

SEED SUPPLIERS

BCS, BPC, HS, NN, PSEU, PZW

USAGE

In India, the pods are used green to make curries and chutneys when fresh and, once ripe, they are dried and processed into chili powder.

This was developed from the crossbreeding of two other Indian chili varieties, NP 46A and the Puri Red. These long, wrinkled chilies are one of the most popular commercial varieties grown in Andhra Pradesh, one of India's major chili-growing areas.

The plants can be more than 3 feet 3 inches high and produce a large crop of pods. In cool, temperate climates, these need to be grown in a hoop house and, unless you have a large hoop house, I do not recommend trying to grow these at home. Instead, look for them dried or fresh at Indian supermarkets.

If you do want to grow some Pusa Jwala, the dried pods are a great source of seeds. Seeds collected in this way are not always the most viable, because they won't have been stored in ideal conditions, but you will get a lot of seeds to try to germinate and you only need a few to grow.

SCOVILLE RATING

30,000–50,000 SHU

56 Sibirischer Haus Paprika

SPECIES

C. annuum

POD DESCRIPTION

Erect, skyward-pointing, short, 1- by ¾-inch blunt pods that mature from dark green to red.

GROWING INFO

The ideal indoor flowerpot plant; move the chili outside in the summer and it should last many years.

SEED SUPPLIERS

SLP

USAGE

Dried and ground to powder.

This is a fast-producing variety and a rarity outside Siberia. The name translates as "Siberian house pepper." The variety has been developed to produce peppers in poor light conditions and is less susceptible to cool conditions.

The compact plant produces an abundance of pods. Siberia has little in the way of commercial chili development, so I suspect this has evolved by growers selecting seeds from successful plants and passing them on to other growers, who have, in turn, done the same.

Sibirscher Haus Paprika makes an ideal flowerpot plant and will do well on a windowsill not in direct sunlight. It is reported that they overwinter well and can last many years.

When dried and ground to a powder, they are used in local dishes, such as *Gulaš* (goulash) or *Perkelt*, a pork and paprika stew.

SCOVILLE
HEAT UNITS

30,000–50,000
SHU

57 Tabasco

SCOVILLE
RATING

30,000–50,000
SHU

This chili gets its name from the Mexican state of Tabasco, and has been made famous as the main ingredient in Tabasco Pepper Sauce, probably the best-known chili sauce in the world.

The production of Tabasco Pepper Sauce dates back to 1868, when Edmund McIlhenny started selling his sauce to the public. The sauce was based on his locally grown Tabasco chilies, which are picked when ripe and ground to a pepper mash before having salt added and then sealed in oak barrels to mature. The maturing process can take up to 3 years, then the Tabasco mash is combined with vinegar before finally being put into bottles and sold.

If you are growing these and don't want to emulate Edmund McIlhenny, then use them to make a great fresh salsa. Just seed and then finely chop up 4 to 5 ripe Tabasco pods and add to 8 to 10 chopped fresh tomatoes. Then add a chopped, seeded sweet pepper, a crushed clove of garlic, and the juice of a lime. Finally, add some chopped fresh cilantro and a little salt and black pepper to taste, and you will have a simple, tasty salsa in just a few minutes.

POD DESCRIPTION

The conical, upward-pointing pods will grow to about 2 inches long and ½–¾ inch wide, maturing from green to yellow to red. They can be used at any stage, but it is traditional to wait for the pods to turn red, and this also is when they are at their best both for flavor and heat.

GROWING INFO

A popular chili to grow, seeds are available almost everywhere. The plant likes a good sunny position and moist soil; watering every other day should be sufficient. If conditions are right, it can produce a heavy crop of pods.

SEED SUPPLIERS

BCS, BPC, BS, CCN, CH, CSB, HS, LS, NMSU, NN, PBPC, PSEU, PZW, SLP, SS, SSS, TCPC, TF, TWF, VNG

USAGE

The main ingredient in Tabasco Pepper Sauce.

58 Dundicut

Apparently the Dundicut is the national pepper of Pakistan—so important is it to the national cuisine—however, it seems it has not yet made it to the growing list of producers in other countries. Pakistan is one of the world's largest producers of chilies, with an annual production of 100,000 tons. It seems that this chili is most commonly grown to make chili powder, probably because of its bright red color.

In countries other than Pakistan, you can find dried Dundicut chilies in specialty Pakistani stores and online at specialty spice companies. I have only seen them sold with the stem removed and, in fact, one supplier lists *Dundicut* as meaning "stemless," which may also be why they are popular to process to powder.

Seeds have not commonly been available, but a few suppliers are now stocking them. If you can source any, try growing some to see what they taste like fresh. It is one I cannot wait to try.

SCOVILLE RATING

30,000–65,000 SHU

59 Goat Horn Pepper

This chili originates from Thailand. It is a nice, compact plant that can grow 2–3 feet tall. In cool, temperate climates, it is best grown in a greenhouse or hoop house, because it is a late developer when it comes to getting the chilies completely ripe.

The long, tapering, slender pods are often described having a Cayenne style because they share a similar shape, but they do not have the distinct, black pepper flavor of the Cayenne (see page 96).

Matt Simpson at Simpson's Seeds (see page 223) makes a sweet smoky Horny Goat Sauce using the Goat Horn Chili. He describes the plant as a high-yielding chili with a good flavor.

Note that there is also an Italian pepper from the Abruzzo region called the Corno Di Capra, or "Goat Horn" in English. This is a much milder pepper, at about 2,000 SHU.

SCOVILLE RATING

35,000–50,000 SHU

60

Bacio di Satana

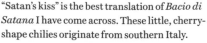

C. annuum

POD DESCRIPTION

The cherry-shape pods grow to 1 inch in diameter, starting lime green and turning scarlet red when mature.

GROWING INFO

This is a good chili to grow, even for the novice. It grows to about 17½ inches high, likes full sun, and would be ideal in a sun room or greenhouse in cool, temperate climates. It produces a consistently high yield of pods.

SEED SUPPLIERS

NN

AKA

Ciliegia Piccante.

"Satan's kiss" is the best translation of *Bacio di Satana* I have come across. These little, cherry-shape chilies originate from southern Italy.

The pods grow facing the sky, making an interesting-looking display. They are thick fleshed and, with the stem and seeds removed, are ideal for stuffing. You may find them in Italian delicatessens stuffed with a mixture of tuna, anchovies, and capers and then stored in olive oil.

I have used these chilies to make chili sherry. Many years ago, the late Peter Seymour (aka Chilli Pepper Pete) introduced me to his sherry recipe, which, like most good ideas, is simple but tastes great. The sherry makes a great drink on cold winter days.

You will need a bottle or two of sherry. The better the sherry you use, the more drinkable it will be. You need to cut slits in the chilies to let the sherry in, then cover the chilies in sherry and store in an airtight container in the refrigerator for a few weeks. Then strain the sherry mixture back into the sterilized sherry bottles, saving the chilies to make a chili mash, which you do by pushing the reserved chilies through a strainer to remove the seeds. Store the resulting mash in an airtight container in the refrigerator and use it to spice up stir-fries, etc.

SCOVILLE
RATING

40,000–50,000
SHU

61

Super Chili F1 & Super Tramp

SPECIES

C. annuum

POD DESCRIPTION

Pods are 2½ –3¼ inches long and ¾ inch wide and ripen from light green to red.

GROWING INFO

My absolute first recommendation for the novice chili grower, it is especially easy to grow, produces excellent usable pods, and is a reliable cropper. I grow mine on a sunny part of the patio in a gardener's grow bag every year. You will not be disappointed.

SEED SUPPLIERS

PSEU, SS, SSS, VNG

Super Chili has the appearance of what many people would consider to be an "ordinary chili," thus it is what people expect when they think "chili." However, despite this, it has a place in any chili grower's top ten list because it is truly an exceptional variety. The particular features that give it its elevated place are its earliness and reliability.

This is the variety recommended to beginners: it is a good germinator, forgiving in less than perfect conditions, fast growing, and will produce copious yields of hot pods.

Being an F1 hybrid variety from the United States, it is easier to get in this country, but availability can be an issue to growers elsewhere.

A new variety called Super Tramp is a product of dehybridizing (see page 8) Super Chili. Over many generations, it has been developed as an open-pollinated variety (see page 8) that has all the characteristics of Super Chili. It looks identical to Super Chili, has all the positive characteristics, but by not being an F1 hybrid, saved seeds, if not crossed with others, will remain true to the variety.

SCOVILLE
RATING

40,000–50,000
SHU

62 Purple Haze

SPECIES

C. annuum

POD DESCRIPTION

Cayenne-style pods (see page 96) grow to 2¾–3¼ inches long and ½ an inch thin, tapering to a point. The pods turn from green to purple at an early stage. Even the stems and calyces are purple and, as the pods ripen, they start to turn a dark red.

GROWING INFO

The plant likes a large container or to be grown in the ground. This is a sprawling plant that will need support once it starts to crop.

SEED SUPPLIERS

CF, SSS

USAGE

These are not the hottest chilies, but try them in a salsa for an unusual color combination. The full heat does not develop until they are ripe, but I like using them when they are purple in chutneys and pickles. I have also dried them, and they retain their color well.

This plant is described as having an "old-fashioned" open-growth habit, which in layman's terms means it is not particularly compact. Because it has a lot of branches, it needs room to grow and, therefore, is not suitable for small flowerpots. Having said that, it is a beautiful plant with lilac-purple flowers, leaves, and stems.

If you have the space, this is an interesting variety to grow just for the color. Purple has become a fashionable color for vegetables and a quick search of the Internet will turn up a carrot also called Purple Haze. There are even some claims that the purple color in foods is good for your memory. I have just remembered that 1967 song "Purple Haze," by Jimi Hendrix, so my memory is working.

SCOVILLE RATING

50,000–75,000
SHU

63 Cheiro Roxa

SPECIES

C. chinense

POD DESCRIPTION

The pods are 1 inch in diameter, and they start off dark purple and mature to lighter purple.

GROWING INFO

This unique looking chili is easy to grow but can take a while to completely ripen.

SEED SUPPLIERS

CCN, NN, PBPC, SLP, UKCS, VNG

USAGE

Ideal for a chutney or pickle once seeded (this may be a little fussy).

Coming from Brazil, the Cheiro Roxa (*Roxa* is Portuguese for "purple") is a most unusual pepper, looking a little like the pod has been compressed so that the middle bulges out.

The pods start dark purple before ripening to a light purple, sometimes with light pink streaks. The plants are tall, growing up to 3 feet 3 inches high, and have purplish green leaves. They crop well, producing a lot of pods.

At 50,000–100,000 SHU, this is a hot variety, but along with that heat there is a little sweetness to the flavor.

SCOVILLE RATING

50,000–100,000 SHU

64 Coffee Bean

SPECIES

C.chinense

POD DESCRIPTION

Round pods that grow
to ¼–½ an inch in
diameter, starting green
before turning bright
orange and then shiny
red.

GROWING INFO

This is a bushy plant
and the size it grows
to will depend on the
size of container you
use. Ideally a 1-quart
flowerpot will produce
a nice compact plant
suitable for the
windowsill. A good
reliable pollinator for
the beginner.

SEED SUPPLIERS

SSS

This is another unusual Habanero variety and
the original seeds are suspected to come from
Central America. About 15 years ago, some
of these seeds came into the hands of Joy and
Michael Michaud of Sea Spring Seeds, who
grew them and named the chili the Coffee Bean,
because when completely ripe, the pods have the
look of coffee berries.

The pods have a noticeable fruity aroma,
which is matched by their flavor. The round pods
grow to ¼–½ inch in diameter, starting green
before turning bright orange and then, finally,
when completely mature, they become shiny red.

If you are looking for a Wiri Wiri chili, then
this makes a good, if a little milder, alternative.
The pods are so small and compact that cutting
them is not always a good option and Joy
recommends just crushing them with the back
of a knife when used in cooking.

I would try pickling some whole or adding
them to some picked onions to give an extra bite.

**SCOVILLE
RATING**

35,000–40,000
SHU

65 Tepin & Pequin

SPECIES

C. annuum

POD DESCRIPTION

Tepin pods are especially small and berrylike at ¼–½ an inch in diameter. Pequin pods are slightly more elongated.

GROWING INFO

Both varieties can be hard to germinate and may require a long time in a warm propagator (77°F +) before they burst into life. Once growing, they can reach 3 feet 3 inches–6 feet 6 inches high. They are not for the novice, but if you can get hold of some seeds, try them out. Tricks for success include slightly scarifying the seeds (cutting the seed coat to encourage germination) to replicate the conditions of being digested by a bird, or growing them in sandy, free-draining soil.

SEED SUPPLIERS

BPC, CF, CH, CSB, HS, LS, NMSU, PBPC, PZW, SLP, VNG

AKA

Bird Pepper.

These are wild chilies (see page 7) that can be found in Mexico and the southern U.S. states of Arizona, Texas, and New Mexico. It is said that with the right conditions, the plants can live for up to 50 years.

Tepin is the Nahuati (Aztec) Mexican word for "flea," which is ideal for such a small chili with such a big bite. The plant can produce an amazing number of pods, but these pods are tiny and more like berries.

A similar pepper called Pequin (which means "small" or "tiny") is normally slightly more elongated than the round Tepin. Both these peppers probably share a common ancestry, because they are both wild peppers and grow in the same regions. The Pequin grows wild but is often harvested, dried, and then sold in the local markets. A few online stores can provide both seeds and pods.

These peppers may also be known as the Bird Peppers and, under this name, variants can be found in places as far south as Argentina and spreading into the West Indies.

SCOVILLE
RATING

50,000–250,000
SHU

66 Ají Cereza

SPECIES
....
C. annuum

POD DESCRIPTION
....
These pods grow
to ¾–1¼ inches in
diameter. They mature
from green to red.

GROWING INFO
....
Can grow to 3 feet high
and needs warmth;
grown in a hoop house
or greenhouse in cool,
temperate climates.

SEED SUPPLIERS
....
PBPC, SLP

USAGE
....
Pods dry well and can
be seeded and pickled
or stuffed with cheese
and roasted.

Cereza means "cherry" in Spanish and *ají* means "pepper" or "chili," so the name of this variety translates as "Cherry Pepper." Ají Cereza is a small, roundish red pepper (much like a cherry) from the jungles of Peru. The pods start green and mature to red and, being thin-fleshed, they dry well. They are well-packed with seeds, and if you carefully cut out the stem and remove the seeds, they can then be easily pickled or stuffed with cheese and roasted.

Ají Cereza are not normally grown commercially, but they are available dried via specialty retailers, in which case they look like a smaller version of the Cascabel (see page 42), if a little lighter in color and with a lot more heat.

SCOVILLE
RATING

60,000–80,000
SHU

67 Murupi Amarela

SPECIES

C. chinense

SCOVILLE
RATING

60,000–100,000
SHU

Coming from the north of Brazil is the Murupi Amarela, which is often described as looking like a distorted and wrinkled finger, with its indentations and slight curvature. But its main claim to fame is its light green color, which turns creamy white as it matures before finally turning light yellow.

You will see a number of chilies called Ají or Chili Amarela, because *amarela* is the Portuguese word for "yellow." They have a sweet, lemon-citrus flavor along with the heat, a sign that this is definitely a *Capsicum chinense*.

The pods start off light green and become creamy white before they mature to light yellow; they are about 2½ inches long and ¾ of an inch wide.

GROWING INFO

A compact plant that is a good producer. Seeds for this chili are not widely available.

SEED SUPPLIERS

PBPC, PSEU, RFC, UKCS

USAGE

With its distinctive, almost white color, this would make a very interesting chili powder or a single-variety sauce.

68 Ají Pinguita de Mono

SPECIES

C. baccatum

SCOVILLE
RATING

70,000–80,000
SHU

I have included this chili just because I love the name. I am told the name translates from Portuguese to "little monkey's penis" or "little monkey's dick."

A native of the jungles of Peru, they can be found described as both *Capsicum baccatum* and *C. annuum*, but I suspect it is a case of different chilies that look similar sharing the same name. Once removed from the plant, chilies are hard to categorically identify. Generally, the majority of chilies called Ají are *C. baccatum* (meaning "berrylike") and they have a slightly sweeter taste, but the *C. annuum* (misleadingly, meaning "annual") has such a variety of pod shapes it is easily misidentified without seeing the original plant and flowers.

POD DESCRIPTION

The pods only grow to about 1½ inches long and ¾ of an inch wide, and they gently taper to a rounded tip. The pods ripen from green to red.

GROWING INFO

A small plant, growing to about 1 foot 8 inches high, it likes full sun and a warm environment. In cool, temperate climates, move it indoors well before any frost if you want to overwinter it.

SEED SUPPLIERS

HS, SLP

AKA

Mono Pinguita, Pipi Mono.

69

Apache F1

SPECIES

C. annuum

POD DESCRIPTION

The wide, conical pods, 1¼ inches long and ¾ inch wide, ripen from light green to bright red.

GROWING INFO

This is a great novice plant that can be grown in a large flowerpot and does not need constant maintenance. You can grow them in a flowerpot on the windowsill or in a sun room in cool, temperate climates.

SEED SUPPLIERS

BPC, NN, SDCF, SLP, SS

This is a beautiful, small, compact chili plant that grows to just 14–17½ inches high and produces loads of small, wide, conical pods that ripen from light green to bright red. Pick them as they ripen and this will keep the plant productive.

Unlike many other smaller ornamental chili plants, this one is not only hot but also tastes just as you expect a chili to taste, with no bitter aftertaste—just sweet, hot, and savory.

The little pods are packed with seeds, but unfortunately, as an F1 variety (see page 9), seed saving will not get you the same variety if you grow them the next year.

These have won a Royal Horticultural Society Award of Garden Merit in Great Britain, which recognizes its excellence for ordinary use, availability, and stability. Seeds are available almost everywhere.

SCOVILLE RATING

70,000–80,000 SHU

Turtle Claw & Submarine

C. chinense

POD DESCRIPTION

Turtle Claw: Small, knobby, elongated pods, 1¼–1½ inches by ½ an inch, that ripen to a pale yellow. Submarine: Pods are 1½ inches long and ¾ of an inch wide and ripen to bright yellow.

GROWING INFO

Both the Turtle Claw and the Submarine grow well in cool, temperate climates in a greenhouse or hoop house. They are both productive and can be grown in a large flowerpot.

SEED SUPPLIERS

PSEU, SLP, SSS

The Turtle Claw chili, which is a most unusual-looking Habanero variety, produces small, elongated pods that ripen from lime green to a pale, almost white, yellow.

The flavor is definitely a Habanero, but with a more pronounced lemony citrus combination that is great for making a fruity hot sauce.

It is known in some regions as the Aribibi Gusano (*gusano* is Spanish for "worm"), but the name I like best is Caterpillar Pepper. If you look at a bunch of pods together, they genuinely look like caterpillars or grubs. This is not the easiest of seeds to germinate, but well worth the attempt.

The Submarine is a new variety from Sea Spring Seeds (see page 223), which was developed from the Turtle Claw in an attempt to make it a more commercial success. It is a larger plant with a higher yield and the pods are more substantial, with a more intense flavor and a small bump in heat to 135,000 SHU. Most significantly, the pods ripen to a pleasing, bright lemon yellow.

If you grow either of these varieties, you will not be disappointed. There is always someone working on a chili or pepper variety to try to improve it, and the Submarine is one example of this ongoing development.

SCOVILLE RATING

70,000–135,000 SHU

71 Thai Dragon

SPECIES

C. annuum

POD DESCRIPTION

This is a great early variety that can produce hundreds of 2–3¼-inch-long slender pods per plant. The pods start dark green and mature to a bright red.

GROWING INFO

Another must-grow chili that is always a good producer of usable pods, it is successful in a gardener's grow bag, large flowerpot, or in the ground. It likes the sun and is excellent in the greenhouse in cool, temperate climates. Highly recommended for the novice grower.

SEED SUPPLIERS

CB, CH, NN, PSEU, SLP, TF, TWF

USAGE

Being thin skinned, pods are ideal for drying and making flakes or powder.

This is one of the first chilies I ever grew, with the Super Chili (see page 134), and both of these will always be found on my growing list. In 2006, the Royal Horticultural Society in Great Britain grew these as part of a trial of 51 chili pepper varieties. Eighteen of the submitted varieties, including my favorites—the Thai Dragon and the Super Chili—received a much coveted Royal Horticultural Society Award of Garden Merit.

I grow these to make my own hot version of Thai sweet chili sauce, using garlic, sugar, sherry vinegar, and ketchup. I'd never go back to the sugary commercial stuff again.

SCOVILLE RATING

75,000–100,000
SHU

72 Prairie Fire

SPECIES

C. annuum

POD DESCRIPTION

Upright pods that are ¾ of an inch long and a ¼ inch in diameter. They start off pale yellow and then turn orange and, finally, red.

GROWING INFO

An ideal plant for a flowerpot because it is small and compact. They are easy to grow and even when completely loaded with pods will not need support.

SEED SUPPLIERS

NN, PSEU, SDCF, SLP, SSS, TCPC, TWF, VNG

USAGE

An excellent and colorful ornamental houseplant.

Prairie Fire has a few meanings to chili enthusiasts. It is not only a variety of chili, but also the name given to a drink laced with hot sauce. This drink started as the forfeit for losing a bet, the original being a whiskey with Tabasco sauce added, but over the years other sauces and alcoholic drinks have been substituted, with the concoction sometimes even being set on fire before being downed in one gulp.

The Prairie Fire chili is a low-growing, multi-branching variety that produces hundreds of small, upright pods that sit above the foliage.

Its low stature makes this variety perfect as a houseplant, with the upright nature of the colorful pods making it attractive. As houseplants, if kept away from cold conditions, they can last for many years, producing more pods each year.

Described as an ornamental, the pods of this chili are not the most tasty, but they can be added to dishes to give a quick buzz of heat. Being small and thin-fleshed, they dry well, and you will see dried pods like these for sale in grinders, so this could be a source for replacement pods.

SCOVILLE RATING

80,000–100,000 SHU

73 Siling Labuyo

POD DESCRIPTION

The pods stand erect from the stems, growing to 1–1½ inches long and ½ inch wide. Most local varieties ripen from green to red, but there are also varieties that ripen to yellow and purple.

GROWING INFO

Likes it warm and humid, so in cool, temperate climates, this is a greenhouse- or hoop house-only variety.

SEED SUPPLIERS

BPC, TWF

AKA

Chileng Bundok, Katumbal, Kitikot, Pasitis, Pasite, Rimorimo, Siling Bundok, Siling Kolikot, Siling Palay, Silit-diablo.

This is a small, Tabasco-type chili (see page 126) from the Philippines. Translated from Tagalog, one of the languages of the Philippines, *Labuyo* is "wild" and *Siling* is "chili," so in English this means "wild chili." A Philippine chocolate company makes a dark chocolate flavored with Siling Labuyo. This is on my must-try list when I can get hold of a bar.

This chili has been added to the Slow Food Foundation Ark of Taste (see page 9) because it is being overshadowed by imported Bird's Eye chilies (see page 166), which are larger, milder, and, unfortunately, cheaper.

This chili makes an excellent sweet chili sauce and it takes only a few minutes. Put ½ cup of water, 1¼ cups of granulated sugar, and ¾ cup of white wine vinegar into a saucepan and bring to a boil, then simmer to reduce to a syrup (10 minutes should do). Meanwhile, finely chop 40 to 50 Siling Labuyo chilies, add to the syrup, and continue to simmer while stirring for 2–3 minutes. Pour into a sterilized jar and store in the refrigerator once cooled, or use it immediately (I normally cannot resist and have to make twice as much as I need).

SCOVILLE RATING

80,000–100,000 SHU

74 Wiri Wiri

SPECIES

C. frutescens,
C. chinense

POD DESCRIPTION

The pod size varies, but
typically it is ½–¾ an
inch in diameter and
matures from light green
to red.

GROWING INFO

Will grow to 1 foot
8 inches tall, produces
a lot of small pods, and
likes warm, consistent
temperatures. A definite
greenhouse or hoop
house variety in cool,
temperate climates.

SEED SUPPLIERS

SSS

USAGE

Used to make pepper
sauce in their native
Guyana.

On asking where Guyana is, I was given a lot of strange answers, but it is in the north of South America just above Brazil, with Suriname to the east and Venezuela to the west. About 80 percent of the country is still untouched Amazon forest, and it is from here that the Wiri Wiri chili originates.

The compact Wiri Wiri plant produces a small, round, cherry-shape pod.

I have seen it described as both *Capsicum frutescens* and *C. chinense* and both statements are to some degree true. Both these species probably shared the same common ancestors and some people think that these two species should be combined.

In their native Guyana, the most popular use for these pods is to make a pepper sauce. Large numbers of them are chopped finely and added to mango flesh, distilled white vinegar, plenty of garlic, and salt, then blended together. The salt and vinegar preserve them by increasing the acidity. However, the sauce is not cooked, so make it in small batches, as needed, because it will not keep.

SCOVILLE
RATING

80,000–150,000
SHU

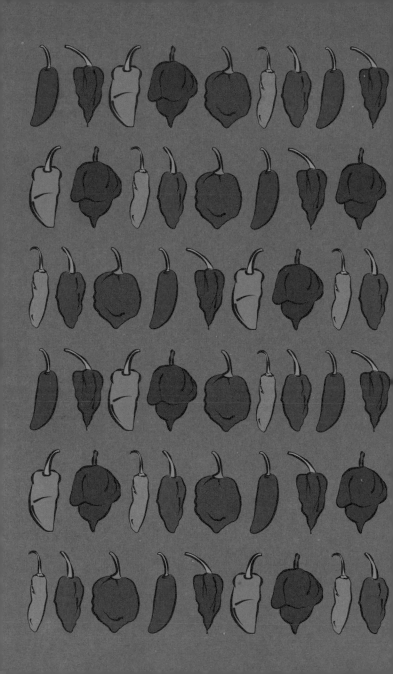

Hot

Goronog

SPECIES

C.chinense

POD DESCRIPTION

The smooth-skinned pods are 2½–3¼ inches and start a light green, turning to a light yellow and finally to a deep yellow-orange. They can grow into unusual, twisted shapes.

This is a Malaysian variety of Habanero, and although it has a smooth skin, it can produce some of the most twisted shaped pods that I have seen, with deep contours and crevices. Milder than most of the other Habaneros listed in this book, with the exception of the Apricot (500–700 SHU) and Zavory (0 SHU), at about 100,000 SHU, this is much hotter than the Jalapeño that most people know, which ranges from just 2,500 to 10,000 SHU.

What makes this a recommended variety is the exceptionally tasty, sweet, and fruity citrus flavor, and the abundance of pods this relatively easy-to-grow plant can produce. The 2½–3¼ inch-long pods start a light green and then turn a light yellow, but as they mature, they take on a much deeper yellow-orange hue.

You will see them listed in seed catalogs as the Malaysian Goronong or Cili Goronong, *Cili* being the Malaysian for "chili," but I have also found them called Caronong or Coronong.

Use these to make a fresh salsa, with a few yellow tomatoes, finely chopped sweet onions, and some cilantro—hot but yummy.

GROWING INFO

Will grow to 2 feet wide and 2 feet high and grows well in a large container. It likes a sunny position but is best grown in a hoophouse or greenhouse in cooler climates.

SEED SUPPLIERS

CCN, SLP, TWF

AKA

Malaysian Goronong, Cili Goronong.

SCOVILLE RATING

100,000–150,000 SHU

76 Bird's Eye

SPECIES

C. annuum

SCOVILLE
RATING

100,000–200,000
SHU

The Bird's Eye chili is not a single variety, but it is a popular name for a style of chili found commonly all over Africa and Asia.

The common factors in the Bird's Eye chilies seem to be their small, compact size and their color. Varieties range from ½–1¼ inches in length and ¼–½ an inch in width, tapering to a point. All of them are thin-skinned and mature from green to red. This description could cover hundreds of varieties and, so it seems, it does.

There is no register for chili names, so a good name seems to stick and may get used again and again. I have seen them listed as *Capsicum annuum*, *C. frutescens*, and even as *C. chinense* (see page 6).

Of the many chilies listed as Bird's Eye, I would look for the African Bird's Eye chili, often just called Piri Piri or Pili Pili, which in Swahili translates to "pepper pepper."

The African Bird's Eye chili has a small pod, no bigger than ¾ of an inch long and ½ an inch wide. The pods point skyward from this bushy plant, which can grow to more than 3 feet 3 inches high, but it seems to also do well confined in flowerpots, if needed.

So if a recipe calls for Bird's Eye chilies, just pick one that is small and fiery, and you won't go too far wrong.

POD DESCRIPTION

The pods will grow to ½–1¼ inches long and ¼–½ an inch wide, tapering to a point. They mature from green to red.

GROWING INFO

A simple variety to grow. They expect a warm, sunny environment and are often grown in sun rooms.

SEED SUPPLIERS

Almost every supplier has some kind of chili that they call a Bird's Eye, so take your pick.

AKA

African Bird's Eye, African Devil, Bird's, Boonie Pepper, Cabe Rawit (Indonesian), Cengek (Sudanese), Cengis (Banyumasan), Cili Padi (Malay), Congo Chili, Kanthari Mulagu (Malayalam), Kochchi (Sinhalese), Ladâ, Lombok Rawit (Javanese), Mombassa Chili, Pequin Chili, Phrik Khi Nu (Thai), Piri Piri, Siling Labuyo (Tagalog/Filipino), Thai Dragon, Thai Hot, Uganda Chili, Zanzibar Chili.

77

Prik Kee Nu

POD DESCRIPTION

Small pods that grow to
¾–1¼ inches long.

GROWING INFO

Likes it hot and humid
and will produce a
large plant covered in
pods if you can get the
conditions right. It does
not like big changes in
temperature.

SEED SUPPLIERS

CB, CSB, HS, PBPC,
PSEU, SLP

This tiny, fiery chili comes from Thailand and is also found in Indonesian and Malaysian cuisine. It is much shorter and a lot hotter than the better-known Thai Hot chili or Bird's Eye (see page 166). The name can be translated as "mouse shit chili" (*prik* = "chili," *kee* = "shit," and *nu* = "mouse"). Don't be put off by the name; it best describes the size and shape of the chilies, not the taste.

When grown in a large flowerpot, it will reach 1 foot 8 inches–2 feet high and produces a mass of small pods. This is not the easiest chili to grow in cooler climates, unless you have a hoop house, because its native climate is humid and warm. A good alternative can be the Rooster Spur, a smaller, more manageable plant.

Prik Kee Nus are the small, whole pods you find in tom yum soup, and they are also used to make nam phrik sauce (which means "fluid chili"). This is simple to make and is used liberally as a condiment with rice and noodles.

To make a simple nam phrik sauce, finely slice 10 Prik Kee Nu chilies and put into a bowl. Peel and crush 2 or 3 garlic cloves and add to the sliced chilies. Add a ½ cup of Thai fish sauce, a ½ cup of lime juice, and 2 teaspoons of packed dark brown sugar and mix well. Store in an airtight container overnight in the refrigerator before use. In Thailand, this would all be done with great skill in a mortar and pestle.

SCOVILLE RATING

100,000–250,000 SHU

78

Bahamian Goat

These mature to a pale orange-peach color and are 1¼–1½ inches wide and 1½–2 inches long. Some will produce a small scorpion-style tail from the base.

Not one of the easiest chilies to germinate, it needs a temperature of 70–73°F and some patience, but once it gets going, it will produce a lot of pods, although these can be slow to finally ripen.

BPC, CH, NN, PZW, SLP, SS, UKCS

Bahamian Goat originates from the Bahamas and looks similar in shape to a Scotch Bonnet (see page 180). The pods mature to a pale orange-peach color. These are similar to the Habanero and can take a long time to germinate, but it's worth it, because the plants grow to about 3 feet 3 inches tall and, in ideal conditions, can produce a heavy crop.

The Bahamas Ministry of Agriculture, Marine Resources, and Local Government has recognized the Bahamian Goat pepper, along with their other local specialty, the Finger pepper, as of special interest, and it has started a process of protection and improvement to increase the hardiness and yield of the crop through careful seed selection. Seeds are also protected in a seed bank as a backup in case of natural disasters.

SCOVILLE
RATING

100,000–300,000
SHU

79

Datil

SPECIES

C. chinense

POD DESCRIPTION

Yellow-orange pods are up to 2½ inches long and 1 inch wide.

GROWING INFO

Some of these plants can last for decades in Florida, and they are prolific producers of pods. They like warm conditions, and in cool, temperate climates this is a hoophouse or greenhouse plant. The seeds can be slow to germinate.

SEED SUPPLIERS

CH, CT, NMSU, NN, UKCS

SCOVILLE
RATING

100,000–300,000
SHU

It is the regional specialities that make chilies so interesting, and unique heritage chilies are now grown around the world. The Datil is one example and has its regional home in St. Augustine, Florida.

The Minorcan community there (originally from the Spanish Balearic Islands) has taken this chili and made it their own. As far as I know, the Datil pepper was not historically grown on the Balearic Islands, so this chili did not do a round trip to Florida via early Spanish explorers.

With its similar heat to the Orange Habanero (see page 178) to which it is probably closely related, the yellow-orange Datil pods grow to 2½ inches long and 1 inch wide.

To survive for hundreds of years, a variety needs a few heroes who grow the plants and collect seeds and create the recipes that use them. In this case, it seems that the dish was the Minorcan Clam Chowder, a fiery, tomato-based chowder that is immensely popular in the St. Augustine area. Recently, the First Coast Technical College in St. Augustine has been growing and selling Datil seeds. In 2007, the Datil Pepper Festival started, with local professional chefs showing off their skills with the Datil chili to win the People's Choice Award.

Whatever its origins, this pepper is moving from a plant grown and known only in Florida to one with a worldwide audience. Seeds are now starting to appear in the online seed catalogs. In 2008, it was included in the Slow Food Foundation Ark of Taste (see page 9), which can only help increase its visibility.

80 Fatalii

SPECIES

C. chinense

SCOVILLE
RATING

100,000–300,000
SHU

A close relation of the Red Savina Habanero (see page 188) and the Scotch Bonnet chilies (see page 180), the Fatalii comes from Central Africa.

Ideal for the first-time grower, the plants grow to about 2 feet tall or more and are easy to grow in full sun. Perhaps I use the term "citrus" too often to describe chilies and, maybe it is the bright yellow of this one that makes me think so, but it has a definite lemon-lime hint to it.

A red variety of Fatalii is also available. This is a natural mutation and some plants will produce both yellow and red peppers at the same time.

POD DESCRIPTION

The pods start green and ripen to a lemon yellow and can grow to 2½ inches long and 1¼ inches wide, tapering to a point.

GROWING INFO

This is a sun lover. In cool, temperate climates, a bright, sunny place in a greenhouse or hoophouse is best. A lot of good-quality seeds are available, giving high germination rates.

SEED SUPPLIERS

BPC, BS, CF, CH, CSB, NN, PBPC, SDCF, SLP, SS, SSS, UKCS

USAGE

A number of excellent sauces make use of this chili.

81 Madame Jeanette

SPECIES
....
C. chinense

SCOVILLE
RATING
....
100,000–350,000
SHU

The Madame Jeanette is a close relation to the Orange Habanero (see page 178) and the Red Savina Habanero (see page 188). This chili may get its name from a professional lady of dubious virtue from Paramaribo, the capital city of Suriname, although others have given her Brazilian nationality. Whatever the truth or lack of it, the chili still packs a punch at up to 350,000 Scoville heat units.

Suriname, officially called the Republic of Suriname, is on the northeastern coast of South America. It was colonized by the Dutch, who governed until 1975, when it became an independent country.

The Suriname Red is also often called the Madame Jeanette, but the pods of the Suriname Red turn red when completely ripe instead of yellow/orange.

POD DESCRIPTION

The pods will grow to 2–2¾ inches long and 1¼–1½ inches wide. They start off light green, then turn a golden yellow and then orange. They look a little more tortured than the Habanero, with a generally more wrinkled appearance.

GROWING INFO

The plants grow to well over 3 feet 3 inches high in the right warm and sunny conditions. Seeds are becoming available for the yellow and red variants, but they are still not common. If you have grown Habaneros successfully, then why not give these a try?

SEED SUPPLIERS

SLP

AKA

Suriname Yellow.

82 Orange Habanero

SPECIES

C. chinense

SCOVILLE
RATING

100,000–350,000
SHU

Anyone who likes heat will know the Orange Habanero. As a Habanero, it is one of the most common and best known. It is also one of the hotter varieties and has been around for a long time, pretty much becoming the standard for Habaneros.

When I started growing chilies, the Red and Orange Habaneros were considered some of the hardest to grow, but as the enthusiasm of the amateur growers for more interesting varieties and the quality of seeds improved, these are now seen as commonplace.

If you want to grow just one type of Habanero, make Orange Habanero the one. Its balance of flavor, heat, and the number of pods produced will pay back your efforts, and more.

POD DESCRIPTION

The lantern-shape pods start dark green and mature to orange, growing to ¾–1¼ inches wide and 1½ inches long. Pick the pods as soon as they are ripe to spur the plant on to producing more.

GROWING INFO

A favorite to grow and popular, there are a lot of good-quality seeds available with high germination rates. The plants are adaptable; when grown in small flowerpots, the plants will be small, although in bigger containers they will be proportionally bigger. In all cases, the variety is productive.

SEED SUPPLIERS

BPC, BS, CF, CH, CSB, HS, LS, MWCH, NMSU, NN, PBPC, PN, PSEU, PZW, RFC, SDCF, SLP, SS, SSS, TF, TWF, UKCS

USAGE

There is a rich supply of recipes from Mexico and the Caribbean and Orange Habanero also makes a great chutney.

83 Scotch Bonnet

SPECIES

C. chinense

SCOVILLE
RATING

100,000–350,000
SHU

These peppers are said to get their name from the tam o'shanter, or Scottish bonnet, historically worn by Scottish men. This chili originated in the Caribbean and it gives jerk dishes their unique heat and flavor. Its connection to jerk cuisine has made this pepper one of the first to be well known around the world—a Jamaican goat curry without Scotch Bonnet is just unthinkable.

Scotch Bonnet is closely related to other Habanero varieties, such as the Red Savina Habanero (see page 188), and has similar heat levels, but it has a different flavor. Over the past few years, a growing number of varieties have been developed and mutated by growers.

West Indian Scotch Bonnet pepper sauce is one of the simplest sauces to make, and each West Indian family probably has its own variation on the recipe. The simplest, and the one I use, has just Scotch Bonnet peppers, salt, and distilled white vinegar blended together and put into sterilized bottles. Do not add too much salt to start. You are trying to make a thin sauce.

POD DESCRIPTION

Traditional pods of this variety will grow to 1¼–1¾ inches long and ¾–1¼ inches wide, ripening from green to either red or yellow, but there are brown and even pink versions, too.

GROWING INFO

Like the Jalapeño (see page 60) and Serrano (see page 88), this is one of the seeds that most suppliers seem to stock. It used to be considered at the difficult end of the growing spectrum, but the increasing quality of the seeds and better knowledge of growing conditions now make this moderately difficult to grow.

SEED SUPPLIERS

BCS, BPC, BS, CB, CF, CH, CSB, HS, LS, MWCH, NN, PBPC, PJ, PSEU, PZW, RFC, SDCF, SLP, SS, TWF, UKCS

AKA

Boabs Bonnet, Bonney Pepper, Caribbean Red Pepper, Scotty Bon.

84 Pimenta de Neyde

SPECIES
....

C. annuum
C. chinense

SCOVILLE
RATING
....

150,000–250,000
SHU

Supposedly named after Neyde Hidalgo, the lady who discovered it growing in her garden in Brazil, the Pimenta de Neyde produces dark purple pods that become a brighter, more luminescent purple as it matures.

The stems and leaves on the plant are also dark purple like the pods. It has long stems and produces a small tree-shaped plant. It is thought to be a cross between a *Capsicum chinense* and a *C. annuum*, but without some genetic work this is just pure speculation.

Seeds are available via speciality suppliers, and, if you have the space, Pimenta de Neyde would be an interesting one to grow and from which to produce additional crosses.

POD DESCRIPTION

The pods will grow to 2½–3¼ inches long, increasing to ¾ inch wide and then narrowing to a rounded tip. Cut open the pods and the inside of the thick flesh and membranes seems almost white in comparison to the skin.

GROWING INFO

The plant grows well, and can reach to more than 2 feet 7 inches tall.

SEED SUPPLIERS

BPC, HS, LS, NN, PSEU, RFC, SLP, TCPC, TWF

85 Peruvian White Habanero

SPECIES

C. chinense

POD DESCRIPTION

The pods start off lime green and turn a creamy white. Each plant can produce an abundance of these little 1¼–2-inch elongated, white pods.

GROWING INFO

You will need to be prepared for a few losses to grow this one, because it likes optimal growing conditions with little variation in warmth.

SEED SUPPLIERS

BPC, BS, CB, CCN, CF, CH, CSB, HS, LS, MWCH, PN, PSEU, RFC, SS, TCPC, TF, TWF

AKA

Yucatán White Habanero.

Although it is probably from Peru, this chili is also known as the Yucatán White Habanero, so it may originate in Mexico. Regardless of its origins, these little, white chili pods pack a hefty punch.

These bullet-shaped pods have been described as "jelly bean-like" by Neil Smith from The Hippy Seed Company (see page 222), and that description could not be more apt.

They are very similar to the slightly smaller Habanero White Bullet® from the Redwood City Seed Company. In the past 10 years, we have seen a profusion of Habanero varieties coming onto the market, providing a range of colors including red, orange, yellow, brown, white, purple, and even black.

Peruvian White Habaneros are notoriously hard to grow, because the plant is particularly susceptible to almost any change from the optimal growing conditions—that is, if you can get a reliable source of seeds that germinate.

They are more often grown for their novelty value than for their flavor, which is slightly citrus. This chili would be good for adding some hidden heat to a white sauce.

SCOVILLE RATING

150,000–300,000 SHU

Devil's Tongue Yellow & Red

C. chinense

POD DESCRIPTION

Devil's Tongue Yellow: Wedge-shaped pods, 1½–2¾ inches long and ¾–1½ inches wide. Devil's Tongue Red: Larger and bright red.

GROWING INFO

Another chili where the germination can be slow; this is a recurring theme with the hotter varieties.

SEED SUPPLIERS

BPC, BS, CH, CSB, HS, NN, RFC, SLP, UKCS

An Amish farmer in Pennsylvania is believed to have originated the Devil's Tongue Yellow. At the right angle, the pods can look like a wrinkled tongue. It has a similar flavor and heat level to an Orange Habanero (see page 178) but has a more wedgelike shape and wrinkled pod. The pods are thin fleshed and grow to 1½–2¾ inches long, depending on how the tongue shape develops, and ¾–1½ inches wide.

The Devil's Tongue Red is said to have been developed from the Devil's Tongue Yellow, but this is pure conjecture, based on the name and shape. It is larger and hotter, with a more sweet, fruity flavor than the yellow variety. With its bright red color, it can look even more like a tongue shape.

Like a lot of these unusual variations, try to buy seeds from a reliable source that has a history of supplying quality seeds. Because most people have never seen these varieties, it is easy to be sold the cheaper and much more common Yellow or Red Habanero seeds. A highly recommended source of these seeds is Jim Duffy of Refining Fire Chiles (see page 223), who grows and sells both the yellow and red varieties.

SCOVILLE RATING

250,000–500,000 SHU

87 Red Savina Habanero

SPECIES

C. chinense

POD DESCRIPTION

The pods will grow to
¾–2½ inches long and
1–1½ inches wide.

GROWING INFO

These used to be
considered hard
to germinate but,
compared to some of
the superhots, they are
a breeze. They do like
warm conditions, but not
always direct sunlight.
The plants grow to 3 feet
3 inches tall and can
produce 50 pods in a
good season.

SEED SUPPLIERS

BPC, BS, CF, CH, CSB,
HS, LS, MWCH, NN,
PBPC, PJ, PSEU, PZW,
RFC, SLP, SS, TF, UKCS

SCOVILLE RATING

350,000–577,000
SHU

When I first got involved in chilies many years ago, this was the most feared chili. It rated at a seemingly mind-boggling 577,000 SHU and was held in even greater reverence than the Bhut Jolokia (see page 200) and the rest of the million-plus club are today. I still have a bottle of pure Red Savina mash, the processed pulped flesh of the chili, which I keep as a collector's item. Today, I can buy supposedly far hotter chilies in my local supermarket.

The Red Savina held the official Guinness World Record from 1994 to 2007. Originally found growing in a field of Orange Habaneros (see page 178), Frank Garcia of GNS Spices in Walnut, California, harvested the red pods, dehydrated them, and saved the seeds. He selectively bred them to produce larger, heavier, and hotter pods, which achieved the then record-breaking 577,000 SHU in 1994.

The Orange Habanero can get as hot as 350,000 SHU so, at the time, a jump to 577,000 SHU was a big increase. In some recent tests, Sea Spring Seeds, the developer of the Dorset Naga (see page 208), grew as many superhots as they could obtain and had them tested at the end of the season. Not one of the chilies passed 400,000 SHU, and this shows just how variable chilies can be and also the quality of the stabilization of some of the varieties. You may think you are eating a 1.5-million-SHU chili, but it could be that the old Red Savina Habanero is hotter and more consistent.

88 Pink Tiger

SPECIES
....
C.chinense

POD DESCRIPTION
....

This is an unstable variety and pods vary greatly in size, shape, and color.

The Pink Tiger is an interesting hybrid of the Bhut Jolokia (aka the Ghost chili) and the Pimenta da Neyde. As far as my research has found, it is an especially unstable hybrid, with plants producing pods in many different shapes.

I believe the original idea of its producer was to produce a hybrid of the Bhut Jolokia and the Pimenta da Neyde to produce a purple Bhut Jolokia. In 2009, Paolo Fisicaro produced a hybrid of these two that was named the Elisa Pimenta AISPES (AISPES is an Italian nonprofit association that works with professional and novice breeders to collect, preserve, and spread the Solanaceae family, which includes some chilies, tomatoes, and other flowering plants). Work is still ongoing to make this a stable variety.

I suspect the Pink Tiger has come out of the AISPES breeding program. Although it is not a purple Bhut Jolokia, it can produce beautifully variegated pods that grow to 2–3 inches long. The pods start green and quickly turn purple with cream or peach stripes or polka dots. I'm told they are capable of turning red if left for long enough.

The taste of this chili is strongly reminiscent of the Bhut Jolokia, but without the initial searing heat. The only samples I have tried have been much milder than expected, but I have read reports rating them with similar heat levels to the Bhut Jolokia. This is probably due to the great variability of this variety rather than the toughness of my palate.

GROWING INFO

Unstable varieties are always hard to grow, because you never really know what you will be getting. It should grow to between 2 feet and 2 feet 8 inches high and will need a warm and sunny position. It is best in a hoop house or greenhouse in cooler climates.

SEED SUPPLIERS

SLP, TCPC, UKCS

SCOVILLE RATING

400,000–500,000 SHU (estimated)

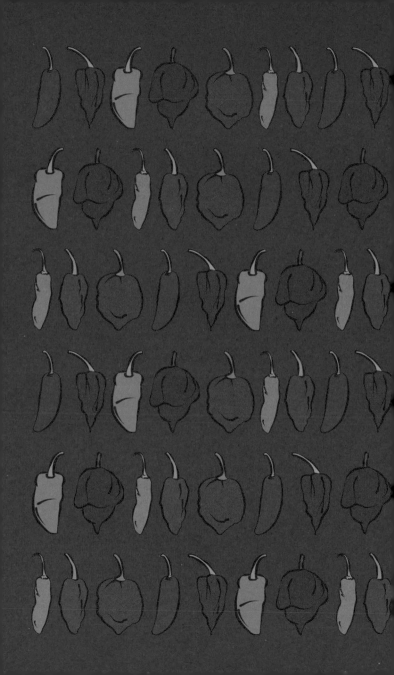

Very
Hot

Nagabon Jolokia
Bubblegum 7 & Borg 9
7 Pot
Bhut Jolokia
Habalokia
infinity
Douglah, Chocolate 7 Pot
Dorset Naga

Nagabon Jolokia

SPECIES

C. chinense

POD DESCRIPTION

The pods will grow to 2–3¼ inches long and ¾–1¼ inches wide.

GROWING INFO

For such a hot pepper, this needs little maintenance. It germinates well and would be a good choice for a novice to grow.

SEED SUPPLIERS

CH, CSB, HS, SLP

A few years ago, The Hippy Seed Company in New South Wales, Australia (see page 222), supplied The Chilli Factory (see page 222) with some Bhut Jolokia seeds. Out of the 500 plants they grew, one was a little different, looking a little more like a Scotch Bonnet (see page 180). This was nicknamed the "Nagabon" (a Naga Bhut Jolokia that looks like a Scotch Bonnet) and The Hippy Seed Company collected some of the seeds and started the process of stabilizing the variety.

Now, Nagabon seeds are available from The Hippy Seed Company and a few other speciality suppliers. The pods are larger than average for a Naga cross, growing to 2–3¼ inches long and ¾–1¼ inches wide, and some weigh more than ¾ ounce. The plant has the look of a Naga and grows to more than 3 feet 3 inches high, but the pods are more Scotch Bonnet-like.

The true ancestry of this chili may never be known, but I love the name and it will forever be linked to the Scotch Bonnet.

SCOVILLE RATING

700,000–800,000 SHU

90 Bubblegum 7 & Borg 9

SPECIES
....

C. chinense

SCOVILLE
RATING
....
250,000–1,000,000
(an estimate; not
officially tested)

These two chilies are included together because they both come from chili enthusiast Jon Harper. He is not a professional grower nor, as far as I know, a geneticist, but he has produced a couple of chilies that have been talked about enthusiastically on the online forums.

The first is the Bubblegum 7, which came from seeds saved from a Moruga Scorpion. The pods produced were larger than expected, the calyx (the base of the flower that then forms the top of the chili, where the stem connects) also produced a surprise. Normally green, this one turned red as the chili ripened. Jon named this one after Bubblicious Bubblegum, which is the taste it reminded him of. When my colleague Chris tried it, bubblegum was the last thing on his mind, because the burn tried to rip out his throat.

The Borg 9 got its name when Jon read that Ernest Borgnine had died, and it seems an apt tribute. It has come from a cross of the Bubblegum 7 and the Naglah, itself a cross of the Naga Bhut Jolokia and the Douglah (see page 206). The Naglah was named by the late Chilli Pepper Pete, otherwise we may have been seeing the Douglabhut, and I don't think anyone wanted that to see the light of day.

You may find some online seed companies selling Jon's creations, but they may not be stable varieties and Jon is still working on these. Chilies are fun to play with because they cross easily, but producing stable varieties can take years, and in many cases this inbuilt instability is what produces the most interesting traits.

POD DESCRIPTION

These can look similar but, with Bubblegum 7, the red color can extend into the larger-than-normal cap and stem. Both varieties have a heavily textured and wrinkled skin.

GROWING INFO

These varieties are for the enthusiast, because they are known as unstable varieties and you cannot be sure of what you will get; germination rates can also be low.

SEED SUPPLIERS

BPC, CF, NN, SLP, UKCS

91   7 Pot

SPECIES
....
C. chinense

SCOVILLE
RATING
....
700,000–
1,200,000
SHU

Originating from Trinidad, the 7 Pot was almost unknown to the world of chili enthusiasts until just a few years ago. The Caribbean Agricultural Research and Development Institute lists this chili as the 7 Pod, but it has become better known to the chili community as the 7 Pot, with the accompanying old wives' tale that it gets this name from its ability to flavor seven pots of stew.

Even in the few years since 7 Pot has emerged, there are already many variations on the theme coming forward. In online seed catalogs, you will find 7 Pot Orange, 7 Pot Burgundy, 7 Pot Yellow, 7 Pot Chaguanas Red (Chaguanas is a town in Trinidad around which this chili was said to originate), Chocolate 7 Pot (see page 206), and 7 Pot Jonah to name but a few. These varieties may be stable, but experience tells me that it can take many years to get a new variety completely stable.

Each color variation is caused by cross-pollination with another variety at some point, and these variations may be stable but only time will tell. Variations occur naturally as plants are cross-pollinated by insects, which is the way we get such a diverse variety of species.

It is probable that all the superhot chilies coming from Trinidad share a common ancestry. Neil Smith at The Hippy Seed Company (see page 222) has been working on a cross between a Yellow Scotch Bonnet and the 7 Pot and has produced what he is calling the NeBru 7 Pot, which has resulted in a pod that matures to yellow. If you hunt around, you will find many other experimental varieties.

POD DESCRIPTION

Similar in shape to a Red Savina Habanero (see page 188) but a little shorter and wider; however, the pod shape can vary with the end being inverted or pointed, some even have a small scorpion tail. In fact, overall these chilies vary considerably; some are almost smooth skinned whereas others have the pimpled skin found on some of the other superhot chilies, with a number of ribs and bulbous segments.

GROWING INFO

Can be hard to germinate, so not recommended for novice growers.

SEED SUPPLIERS

BPC, BS, CF, CH, HS, LS, NN, PBPC, SLP, SS, UKCS

AKA

7 Pod.

Bhut Jolokia

SPECIES

C. chinense

SCOVILLE
RATING

750,000–1,500,000
SHU

In the year 2000, the India Ministry of Defence tested a locally grown chili, known then as the Naga Jolokia (*Jolokia* meaning "chili pepper" and "Naga" from the location of the chilies in Nagaland in the northeastern part of India) at 855,000 SHU.

Then, in 2004, Frontal Agritech, an Indian commercial agricultural company, tested the then-named Bih Jolokia at 1,047,427 SHU. The world record at the time was held by the Red Savina Habanero (see page 188) at 577,000 SHU.

In 2007, researchers at New Mexico State University claimed the world record for heat at 1,001,304 SHU, for what became known as the Ghost chili, which was grown from seeds collected in India in 2001.

Work published by New Mexico State University shows this chili to be a naturally occurring, interspecific hybrid and, although it was mostly *Capsicum chinense*, some traits from *C. frutescens* were also identified in DNA testing.

In Germany in 2011, Guinness World Records recorded a new record for eating three Bhut Jolokia chilies in 1 minute, 11 seconds by Birgit Tack. The record for the most eaten in 2 minutes—2½ ounces—goes to Jason McNabb from the United States on June 19, 2013.

POD DESCRIPTION

The pods will grow to 2–3½ inches long and ¾–1¼ inches wide, generally tapering to a point. The skin is pimpled and rough looking and the pods can look ridged and textured.

GROWING INFO

This is not the simplest chili to grow; it is slow to germinate and needs germination temperatures of 75–82°F. In cool, temperate climates, it needs to be grown in a sunny hoop house or greenhouse. Will also be slow to ripen, but you can eat the pods at any stage.

SEED SUPPLIERS

BPC, BS, CF, CH, CSB, HS, LS, NMSU, NN, SDCF, SLP, SS, UKCS, VNG

AKA

Bhoot Jolokia, Bih Jolokia, Borbih Jolokia, Ghost chili, King Cobra Chili, Malta, Nagahari, Naga Jolokia, Naga Moresh, Naga Morich, Raja Mirchi, U-Morok.

93 Habalokia

SPECIES

C. chinense

SCOVILLE
RATING

800,000–1,000,000
SHU

This is a cross between a Habanero variety and a Bhut Jolokia (see page 200), hence the name Habalokia. As with most of these new chili varieties, there are a lot of varieties that seem to go under this name. I have seen versions called Habalokia Brown, Chocolate Habalokia, Orange Habalokia, and Habalokia Red to name but a few.

These crosses are not considered stable as yet, and the plants can produce pods with erratic shapes and low germination rates, but this does not seem to limit the number of seeds that have become available on the Internet.

Growing unstable varieties can be interesting. To get a stable cross can take many years' work, with the chili plants remaining isolated during flowering and the setting of the pods, or else they may become crossed yet again with other chilies grown nearby.

Growing these can be somewhat of an adventure, because you will never be sure of what you will get.

POD DESCRIPTION

These pods are often wrinkled and a little contorted, with the pimpled skin found on some of the other superhot chilies. They can grow to 2–2¾ inches long and ¾–1½ inches wide at the top, tapering down to a point.

GROWING INFO

One of the hardest to germinate, with many growers reporting little success, which is one of the problems with many unstable varieties.

SEED SUPPLIERS

BPC, LS, UKCS

94 Infinity

SPECIES

C. chinense

POD DESCRIPTION

These have round pods with a slight taper at the bases. The skin is generally wrinkled. Pods are 1¼–1½ inches in diameter.

GROWING INFO

Like most very hot chilies, these can take a while to germinate and expect warm, sunny conditions.

SEED SUPPLIERS

BPC, CF, CH, HS, PSEU, SLP, UKCS

The Infinity chili was discovered by Nick Woods growing in his hoop house in Grantham, Great Britain, among all the other superhot chilies he was growing for his business Fire Foods: "I knew as soon as I saw it in the hoop house. It stood out, and, when I dissected it, I could tell by the skin tissue and the seeds that it was a hot one," said Nick, who thinks it may be an accidental cross between a Trinidad Scorpion (see page 212) and a 7 Pot (see page 198).

My colleague Tony Ainsworth (aka Darth Naga) ate a pod during a tasting in October 2009. The effects were devastating and I believe a video of this can still be found on YouTube.

Nick Woods supplied some seeds to Simpson's Seeds (see page 223) in early 2009 and samples were sent to Warwick University in Great Britain for testing. The result came back at 1,067,286 SHU, and later tests of the 2010 crop increased this result to 1,176,182 SHU.

In March 2010, the Infinity held the Guinness World Record with the original test result of 1,067,286 SHU. The Infinity chili did not hold the record for long. It was surpassed in February 2011 by the Naga Viper (see page 216), but it helped to fire up the race for the record. You may be able to find seeds, but they are now becoming few and far between and, because this variety was an accidental cross, it cannot be expected to be stable.

SCOVILLE RATING

800,000–1,176,182 SHU

95

Douglah, Chocolate 7 Pot

SPECIES
....
C. chinense

The Trinidad Douglah has shot to fame over the past couple of years as being a real contender for the world's hottest chili. Its chocolate brown skin is pimpled and the almost white internal membrane seems to leak capsaicin at the slightest touch.

It seems the Douglah and the Chocolate 7 Pot could be the same beast. Recent tests showed the Chocolate 7 Pot had a peak of 1,853,936 SHU, with an average of 1,169,058 SHU.

There seems to be so many variations on the Douglah/Chocolate 7 pot theme that, without some work on the genetics, we may never know the true provenance of these varieties.

The Douglah pods have a thin, wrinkly skin, starting green and maturing to a chocolate brown. The pods are not easy to germinate and take a long time to mature. In cool, temperate climates, you will need a greenhouse or hoop house and you should get your seedlings started early. This is not a chili recommended for first-time growers. (Out of interest, the word *Dougla* in the West Indies is used to describe a person of mixed African and East Indian descent.)

SCOVILLE RATING

800,000–1,800,000 SHU

96 Dorset Naga

SPECIES
····································
C. chinense

SCOVILLE
RATING
····································

876,000–970,000 SHU
(but 1,598,227 SHU
in BBC tests)

Strangely originating from the Southwest coast of England, Dorset Naga must be one of the few very hot chilies that have not held the world record for heat, but it easily could have done, and could, in fact, still be the record holder today.

Developed by Joy and Michael Michaud of Sea Spring Seeds (see page 223) from the Bangladeshi Naga Morich (fairly unknown outside of the British-Bangladeshi community), the first plants grown in 2002 showed a wide diversity of plant and pod sizes and shapes. The selection process was refined over the following years, resulting in the characteristic wedge shape and finely wrinkled skin of the Dorset Naga.

In 2005, samples tested in New Mexico and New York hit 876,000 SHU and a staggering 970,000 SHU, beating the existing Guinness World Record that was held by the Red Savina Habanero (see page 188) at 577,000 SHU, but the discrepancy between the two seemed so large that the Dorset Naga developers were reluctant to chase the record.

In 2006, it was included in the British BBC television program *Gardeners' World* chili trial. Seeds were sent to growers around the country and the pods sent for testing at Warwick University, where the highest result given for this chili was 1,598,227 SHU. Today, the chili record officially stands at 1,569,300 SHU for the Carolina Reaper chili (see page 220), which was awarded in November 2013, some seven years later.

Although never officially the world record holder, the Dorset Naga is nonetheless one of the world's hottest chilies.

POD DESCRIPTION

These wedge-shaped pods start off green and ripen to red. They can grow up to 2½ inches long, but 1½–2 inches is more typical, and they reach 1¼–1½ inches wide at the shoulders.

GROWING INFO

Given the space, this can grow to be a massive plant. Plants with more than 2,000 ripe chilies have been known. Not for the novice grower but a good introduction to very hot chilies.

SEED SUPPLIERS

BPC, CF, CSB, HS, LS, SSS

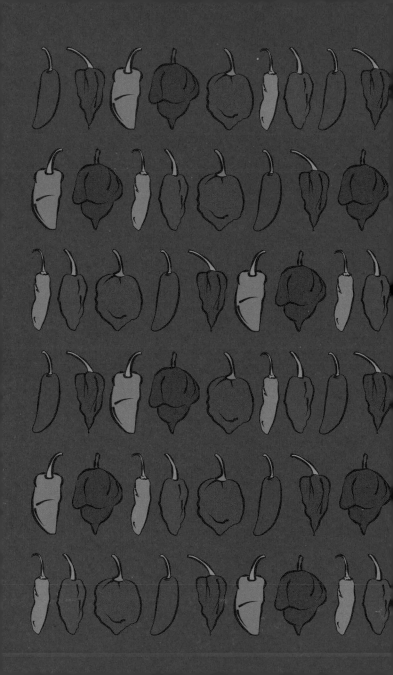

Superhot

Trinidad Scorpion
Fatalii Gourmet Jigsaw
Naga Viper
Katie Habanero
Carolina Reaper (HP22B)

97 Trinidad Scorpion

SCOVILLE
RATING

900,000–1,463,700
SHU

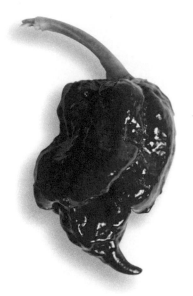

The Trinidad Scorpion gets its name from the sometimes tail at the bottom of the pod. It is uncommon even in its home of Trinidad and in 2009 my friend Joseph McCullough (aka Chilli Joe) spent his month-long vacation in Trinidad hunting for the Scorpion and its cousin the 7 Pot (see page 198). He eventually managed to track them down, but fast-forwarding to 2011 the Trinidad Scorpion came to the notice of the world when a variety called Trinidad Scorpion Butch T was awarded the World Record at 1,463,700 SHU.

Grown and submitted for the record by The Chilli Factory (see page 222), the seeds for this record had been sourced from Neil Smith of The Hippy Seed Company in July 2010 (you may know Neil from his video chili reviews on YouTube). Why is this called the Butch T? Neil called this variety the Butch T because he had obtained the seeds from Butch Taylor of Zydeco Farms, Mississippi, who had been growing and developing chilies for many years.

Alex de Wit at The Chilli Factory tends his chilies with a lot of love and care, giving them the best conditions for growth. Other growers use the "treat-them-mean" technique, depriving them of water after the pods have formed, in the hope the plant will produce more capsaicin to protect the pods as they develop. Research is underway to see how much growing conditions affect heat, but don't expect results for a few years.

The Australian Trinidad Scorpion Butch T held the record until November 2013, when it was beaten by the Carolina Reaper (see page 220), which clocked in at 1,569,300 SHU.

POD DESCRIPTION

The pods can grow to 1½–3¼ inches long, including the sharp pointed tail, and will ripen from green via orange to red. This can take a while in cool, temperate climates.

GROWING INFO

Recommended for only the experienced grower, it is not the easiest chili to grow and there is often the problem of poor germination. This chili expects warm condition—68°F—before the seeds will sprout, and in cool, temperate climates it definitely needs a greenhouse or hoop house and careful attention to see any decent results. It is simpler for this and many of the other superhot chilies to order plug plants from a reputable local supplier.

SEED SUPPLIERS

BCS, BPC, BS, CB, CCN, CF, CH, CSB, HS, LS, MWCH, NMSU, NN, PN, PSEU, PZW, RFC, SLP, TCPC, TF, TWF, UKCS, VNG

98 Fatalii Gourmet Jigsaw

SPECIES

C. chinense

SCOVILLE
RATING

1,200,000 SHU
(an estimate;
no published
results)

This chili comes from the Finnish chili specialist Jukka Kilpinen, who runs the website Fatalii.net. His idea was to try to breed a hotter chili using the Moruga Scorpion chili and crossbreeding it with other superhot chilies.

Chili breeders are well-known for keeping their crossbreeds a closely guarded secret, because a successful record attempt can be worth a lot of money.

After a few years of selectively breeding among just the hottest of the chilies, the Fatalii Gourmet Jigsaw, with its bright red, shiny, contorted skin, was created. When cut open, this thin-fleshed pod reveals an oily inner lining of what I suspect is capsaicin leaking from its membranes.

As far as I have been able to ascertain, there are no published test results for this chili, so the rumor mill has been doing overtime. I have tasted both the Carolina Reaper (see page 220), which is the current world record holder, and the Fatalii Gourmet Jigsaw, and both chilies completely blew me away. As I get older, I don't seem to be getting any wiser—I could not tell you which was the hottest. Both caused complete havoc with my body, leaving me with little memory of any flavor before the heat hit. Others have told me that the flavor is similar to the Bhut Jolokia (see page 200), if a little sweeter and fruitier.

POD DESCRIPTION

Like most of the superhots, the pods have a pimpled skin and a contorted, tapered shape. They can grow to ¾–1¼ inches wide and 1½–2½ inches long.

GROWING INFO

If you can get seeds, then try growing them, but expect long germination times. The pods will also be slow to mature. However, if the plants can be grown successfully in the Finland climate, what have you got to lose?

SEED SUPPLIERS

Seeds are becoming available. Try UKCS and FS for more news of this variety.

99 Naga Viper

SPECIES
....
C. chinense

SCOVILLE
RATING
....
**1,000,000–1,382,118
SHU**

This is another accidental Guinness World Record Holder at 1,382,118 SHU. It was discovered by Gerald Fowler of The Chilli Pepper Company (see page 223) and grown in Cark, Cumbria, in Great Britain. It is described as a three-way hybrid of a Naga Morich (see page 209), Bhut Jolokia (see page 200), and Trinidad Scorpion (see page 212), but I have never been sure how this was achieved.

Unfortunately, its seeds have been a little unstable and do not always produce what is expected. Work is continuing to try to produce a stable version of this variety, but this can take many generations. Some seeds are available, but you may not get what you expect when they produce pods.

The Naga Viper did have a dramatic effect on Gerald Fowler's business. Within a few days of attaining the record, he had huge back orders for the sauce he had made with it and a waiting list for over 1,200 packets of seeds. A record like this brings international recognition and sales, but scaling up the success to meet demand can lead to a lot of customers being disappointed at the speed of delivery.

Growing a chili from seedling stage to the point at which it is mature enough to provide seeds can take 90–100 days. Those seeds then need to be removed from the pod, dried, and tested to make sure they germinate before packing and sending them out to customers. That is no problem if you have produced a stable variety. Stabilization can take many growing seasons and careful plant selection.

POD DESCRIPTION

The pods have wrinkled and contorted flesh with a lightly textured skin. They can grow to 1½–2½ inches long and ¾–1¼ inches wide.

GROWING INFO

Not the easiest to germinate, and probably still unstable, but the plants can produce some stunning pods.

SEED SUPPLIERS

BPC, CF, CH, HS, LS, PJ, PSEU, TCPC, TF, TWF, UKCS

100

Katie Habanero

C. chinense

SCOVILLE
RATING

Possibly 1,590,000
SHU

In late 2014, the British BBC television channel asked if I would appear on a program to act as a chili expert and to discuss this new chili variety. I appeared with Matt Simpson of Simpson's Seeds, a well-known grower of chilies in Great Britain (see page 223), and Tim Woodman from Bath University, England. Tim had produced the provisional test results and had been working with Matt to develop a method of testing using an industrial MRI scanner (not the type the hospitals use).

Both Matt and Tim did not want to push the results of the tests as a new record because they were tests of a small (single-pod) sample, but the results do look promising for the future, although a larger batch would need to be randomly tested.

Matt had obtained the seeds from Nick Duran, a grower based in Somerset, England, nicknamed Naga Nick. Katie is the name of one of his daughters and there is also another Habanero called Lucy after his other daughter. This clocked in at 1,359,284 SHU.

Seeds for both of these superhot chilies are now being sold by a number of seed companies, but, with so many fakes coming to the market, make sure you get an original.

POD DESCRIPTION

Katie Habanero produces large pods, 1½–2½ inches wide, that ripen to a bright red. The plants grow to about 3 feet 3 inches high.

GROWING INFO

Matt Simpson at Simpson's Seeds stressed his crop, removing stems and even shouting at the plants, before picking the chilies for testing. The jury is still out as to whether this worked.

SEED SUPPLIERS

SS, TCPC, UKCS

101 Carolina Reaper (HP22B)

C. chinense

SCOVILLE
RATING

**1,569,000 average–
2,000,000+ peak**

This chili burst on the scene during 2011–12, when it appeared as HP22B. Now named the Carolina Reaper, it was awarded the Guinness World Record in November 2013.

Developed by Ed Currie, owner of PuckerButt Pepper Company (see page 222), this chili was worked on for over 10 years. I believe the chili was scrutinized carefully by the Guinness World Record team after such a quick succession of records had been awarded in the previous few years. Ed tested nearly 45 pounds over three years and provided an 18-page report that included data from chemistry, botany, and biology over a five to eight year period, as well as photographic proof over nine years

Being a brave and now stupid-feeling author, I taste tested this pod, hoping to give you a full account of the flavors. I have eaten a few superhot chilies and some amazingly hot sauces over the years, but I was in over my head with this one—it nearly killed me. A few chews and the rest of my taste test was a blur followed by a lot of milk and ice cream.

Ed tells me it has a sweet, fruity flavor with hints of cinnamon and chocolate, but I never got that pleasure. I have a lot of respect for the chili enthusiasts, including Darth Naga, Nigel Carter, Neil Smith, and Chilli Dave, who record videos, make it to the end of a pod, and can still talk.

News has come in from Ed about his latest creation. Currently only known as the HP56 Death Strain, this may be his next candidate for the record with latest results averaging 2,890,000 SHU.

POD DESCRIPTION

The shape and skin of the pods needs to be seen to be believed; they are contorted with pimples and bulges, before finally the stinger tail protrudes from the bottom. Pods change from light green to a crimson red and, including the tail, they can be 3 inches long and the same wide.

GROWING INFO

Plants can reach to more than 5 feet tall, so you will need a lot of space, and expect a long germination period.

SEED SUPPLIERS

BPC, CB, CCN, CF, CH, CSB, HS, MWCH, NN, PBPC, PN, PSEU, PZW, RFC, SLP, TCPC, TF, TWF, UKCS, VNG

Seed & Plug Plant Suppliers

BCS – Baker Creek Seeds (USA)
www.rareseeds.com

BPC – Buckeye Pepper Company (USA)
www.buckeyepepper.com

BS – Bountiful Seeds (France)
www.bountifulseeds.com

CB – Chillibird (Australia)
www.chillibird.com.au

CCN – Cross Country Nurseries/ChilePlants.com (USA)
www.chileplants.com

CF – The Chilli Factory (Australia)
www.thechillifactory.com

CH – Chillihead.co.za (South Africa)
www.chillihead.co.za

CSB – Chilli Seed Bank (Australia)
www.chilliseedbank.com.au

CSU – Chile Seed USA (USA)
www.chileseedusa.com

CT – Chili Taarn (Denmark)
www.chilitaarn.dk

FS – Fatalii Seeds (Finland)
www.fataliiseeds.net

HS – The Hippy Seed Company (Australia)
www.thehippyseedcompany.com

LS – Livingseeds (South Africa)
www.livingseeds.co.za

MWCH – Midwest Chileheads LLC (USA)
www.midwestchileheads.com

NMSU – NMSU Chile Pepper Institute (USA)
www.chilepepperinstitute.org

NN – Nicky's Nursery Ltd (UK)
www.nickys-nursery.co.uk

PBPC – PuckerButt Pepper Company (USA)
www.puckerbuttpeppercompany.com

PJ – Pepper Joe's (USA)
www.pepperjoe.com

PN – Pepper North (Canada)
www.peppernorth.com

PSEU – Pepperseeds.eu (Netherlands)
www.pepperseeds.eu

PZW– Peperzadenwinkel.be (Belgium)
www.peperzadenwinkel.be

RFC – Refining Fire Chiles (USA)
www.superhotchiles.com

RMR – Reimer Seeds (USA)
www.reimerseeds.com

SDCF – South Devon Chilli Farm (UK)
www.southdevonchillifarm.co.uk

SLP – Semillas La Palma (Spain)
www.semillus.de

SS – Simpson's Seeds (UK)
www.simpsonsseeds.co.uk

SSS – Sea Spring Seeds (UK)
www.seaspringseeds.co.uk

TCPC – The Chilli Pepper Company (UK)
www.thechillipeppercompany.co.uk

TF – Tyler Farms (USA)
www.tyler-farms.com

TWF – Trade Winds Fruit (USA)
www.tradewindsfruit.com

UKCS – UK Chilli Seeds (UK)
www.ukchilliseeds.co.uk

VNG – Victoriana Nursery Gardens (UK)
www.victoriananursery.co.uk

Acknowledgments

Author acknowledgments

Thanks to all the chili enthusiasts that put up with my calls, emails, and visits over the 6 months it has taken to collect and verify the information I needed to write this book. Special thanks goes to Joy Michaud at Sea Spring Seeds and Matt Simpson of Simpson's Seeds, who luckily are based just a few miles from me.

I must also thank my family, who have had to put up with so many visits to chili farms and events over the past decades. So thanks to wife Sonia and the kids, Nick, Jason, Lizzi, Antony, and Mary. Another special thanks to Edna, my mother, without whom there would be a lot more mistakes in the text.

Picture credits

123RF bruno135 2. **Alamy** 67photo 205; Adrian Sherratt 202, 212, 216; Antony Nettle 208; Antony Ratcliffe 182; Banos 39; Clare Gainey 53, 121; franco pizzochero/MARKA 78; Jamie Pham Photography 111; John Glover 57; Keith Mayhew 47; Malcolm Park food images 44; Mim Friday 131; Nikreates 42, 148; OnWhite 176; Rex May 101, 113, 155; Richard Ellis 73; Ryan B. Stevenson 32; Teubner Foodfoto/Bon Appetit 94. **Buckeye Pepper Company** 81, 159, 171. **ChilePlants.com** 69, 83, 85, 99, 107, 139, 185, 187, 19, 23, 67. **chilitaarn.dk** 173. **Chilli Pepper Institute New Mexico State University** 76. **Christopher Phillips** 145, 169. **Dreamstime.com** Anphotos 60; Bert Folsom 20; Bhofack2 63; Daniel Novoa 116; Lucie Lang 180; Lunamarina 88; Mrsixinthemix 220; Msheldrake 48; Ngoc Thu Nguyen Ho 166; Pamela Panella 178, 200; Paulpaladin 96; Pipa100 40, 126; Ppy2010ha 92; Ryan Stevenson 90; Tgshutter 36; Thomas Dutour 65; Vinicius Tupinamba 28; Zigzagmtart 54. **Enrico Lai AKA "The Mojo Pepper"** (**mojopepper.blogspot.com**) 190; **fataliiseeds.net** Jukka Kilpinen 214. **GAP Photos** Heather Edwards 51, 157; Juliette Wade 151; Lynn Keddie 198; Nicola Stocken 31. **Garden World Images** Lee Thomas 119; William Clevitt 133. **Hans-Joachim Baader, www.hjbaader.de** 109. **iStock** Dvdovalina 143; YinYang 74. **Matt Simpson/www.simpsonseeds.co.uk** 27. **Phil Gremillion, Farms of Papa Jeabert, USA** 105. **picturesofus.net** Desmond Johnson 123. **Rep07** 129. **Sea Spring Seeds** 25, 34, 103, 137, 141, 153, 161, 17. **Shutterstock** bonchan 14, swa182 189. **The Garden Collection** FP/Martin Hughes-Jones 13. **The Hippy Seed Company** 195. **Thinkstock** fotoduki 174. **Toms Treibhaus** Thomas Schneider 125. **Tuttodipeperoncini.com** Giancarlo 115. **ukchilliseeds.co.uk** 70, 146, 164, 197, 206, 218. **Victoriana Nursery Gardens** 87. **www.sowchillies.co.uk** 135.